FIRST IN LAW

FIRST IN

LEADERSHIP

William & Mary

Ethical Public Service
The George Wythe Legacy

by

Suzanne Harman Munson

WWW.OAKLEAPRESS.COM

Publisher: The Oaklea Press,

www.oakleapress.com

Author: Suzanne Harman Munson,

www.suzannemunson-author.com

CONTENTS

FOREWORD

After declaring independence in 1776, America faced two crises: an underfunded war against the western world's mightiest military power and a dearth of good leaders in government.

No one had been educated for leadership within a democratic republic, as the country had yet officially to adopt this revolutionary form of self-governance in a constitution. Addressing the urgent need for trained statesmen and jurists, Virginia officials opened America's first law school at the College of William & Mary in 1779.

Those who studied law in Williamsburg during the late-eighteenth century would have a profound and far-reaching influence in assuring that the country's new government would succeed and last beyond the Founding Fathers' lifetimes.

This book focuses on the law school's first decade, which began during the hazardous years of the American Revolution and ended as the new nation adopted its groundbreaking Constitution.

America's first professor of law, George Wythe, played crucial roles in all of the seminal events of the period, modeling for his students the ideal of the honorable Servant Leader. The teaching of ethical conduct in government and the law is essential for every free society.

Principled Servant Leadership remains a core value of the William & Mary Law School today. The school's vision statement underscores this mission: "We serve our communities by leading as passionate, tireless, and ethical advocates who understand the immense responsibilities of the profession and the law's ability to affect society."

Chapter One
The Founding of the Law School
at the
College of William & Mary

"A deficit of adequate statesmen"

James Madison, 1780

From its inception during the height of the Revolutionary War, the William & Mary Law School was planned to produce leaders for an emerging nation.

Contrary to a popular perception, America in the heady days of the Revolution was not filled with legions of Founding Fathers, men of distinction. In fact, depending on who is counting, the number of individuals meriting the title "Founding Father" is fewer than a dozen.

Four years after America declared independence, James Madison wrote to Thomas Jefferson about the country's disastrous condition in the halls of leadership and on the battlefield. In March of 1780, Madison observed that America's finances were bankrupt, public credit exhausted, the army in danger of disbanding, and the fight for freedom in grave jeopardy. The crux of the problem, he reflected, was a "deficit of adequate statesmen."[1]

Earlier, in December of 1778, George Washington had expounded on the leadership crisis in a dispatch to his Virginia colleague Benjamin Harrison, castigating members of the Continental Congress who were serving in governance during the hardest years of the Revolution. Their failure to provide leadership and support for America's liberty had proven catastrophic, he said.

Delegates dithered comfortably in Philadelphia while the Revolution floundered on the front: patriot soldiers were eating their horses for food and marching shoeless on bloody feet in the snow, lacking gunpowder while preparing for combat against England. Profiteering ran out of control, as suppliers chose price-gouging over patriotism.

In the letter to Harrison, Washington observed that America's affairs of state were in a "distressed, ruinous and deplorable condition." Of the leadership, he said that most in the Congress were idle, dissipated, and extravagant, consumed by "an insatiable thirst" for getting rich. He continued: "Party disputes and personal quarrels are the great business

7

of the day while the momentous concerns of an empire are but secondary considerations and postponed from day to day—from week to week." [2]

Between 1774 and 1789, the Continental Congress served as the government of the thirteen American colonies and later of the United States. As hostilities worsened with England, each of the former colonies was tasked with sending qualified delegates to Philadelphia to support the Revolution.

Washington despaired that Virginia's best leaders had left from there by 1778 to take care of affairs at home. "I cannot help asking—Where is Mason, Wythe, Jefferson, Nicholas, Pendleton, Nelson, and another I could name?" He pleaded with Harrison, serving as Speaker of the Virginia House of Delegates, to provide capable representatives for national service:

> *You are beseeched most earnestly my dear Colo. Harrison to exert yourself in endeavoring to rescue your County by sending your ablest and best men to Congress. These characters must not slumber, nor sleep at home, in such times of pressing danger—they must not content themselves in the enjoyment of places of honor or profit in their*

own Country while the common interests of
America are moldering and sinking into irre-
trievable ruin. [3]

In short, Washington asked for servant leaders,
for individuals who would put the welfare of the
country before personal gain and comfort. Some of
Virginia's leaders shared that vision, but ethical, non-
self-dealing public service was not a widespread ideal
in America at the time. As the country freed itself
from the grip of English rule, this vision was yet to
be instilled in future leaders through education.

Few today realize how fragile, how shallow in
bench strength, America's leadership was at the beginning of nationhood. Without the vision and
tenacity of a handful of excellent individuals, the
course of American history could have taken an entirely different, less promising direction.

Except for a small cadre of college-educated
elite, the vast majority of Americans had little or
no formal education during the eighteenth century.
Schools like Harvard, William & Mary, Princeton,
and Yale were founded to train preachers, not
statesmen. No courses existed to teach future leaders to operate capably and ethically within a democratic republic. Technically, America's democratic

republic did not officially exist until the United States Constitution became the supreme law of the nation in 1789, as the definitive operating manual for governing a united country.

It could be asserted that America's first great leadership crisis materialized on July 4, 1776—the day that separation papers were issued to the Mother Country. Until then, Americans had lived under a long-standing, unalterable governing system. A king or queen ruled at the apex of the structure. Parliament made laws for the people. English governors oversaw matters in the respective colonies, and they were free to disband colonial legislatures that showed too much independence.

This governing system was all that the colonists and their ancestors had known for generations. They may have chafed under it, but it was hard to imagine another way of life. On July 4, 1776, all of that familiar structure disappeared. Many feared mob rule when debate ensued about a democratic form of government.

There was talk of enthroning George Washington as the nation's new king. London's leaders were certain that without their superior authority, America's ignorant rabble would soon flounder. The upstart nation's success would be a direct threat to their power at home and abroad. The stakes were high.

Immediately after declaring independence, Virginia's civilian leaders began a rapid transformation of the former English colony into an American state, while fellow Virginian George Washington waged war with an uncertain outcome. Although the Revolution was far from won, Virginians were already acting as if they were free from foreign control.

For Thomas Jefferson, James Madison, George Mason, George Wythe, and other forerunners, the break with England offered unprecedented opportunities for constructive change. In June of 1776, weeks before publication of the Declaration of Independence, Virginia leaders had already begun drafting a new constitution with a declaration of rights, planning a new court system, and instituting other reforms. Other states soon followed suit.

Restructuring Virginia's institution of higher education ranked near the top of the list of corrective measures. Founded in 1693, the College of William & Mary was the second oldest college in America, after Harvard. It served as Virginia's preeminent school of higher learning at the time of the Revolution.

With some exceptions, the college faculty consisted of disgruntled Anglican clergymen. The curriculum, originally created by English authorities and including a school of divinity and theology, was designed to teach religious principles and to provide a proscribed education for the colony's elite. When teachers and administrators departed for England at the outbreak of hostilities, the college was offered a splendid opportunity for transformation.

A new board of visitors convened, reading like a Who's Who of prominent Virginians. It included three of attorney George Wythe's former legal apprentices: Thomas Jefferson, Edmund Randolph, and the Reverend James Madison, second cousin to the future president of the same name and newly appointed president of the school, as well as future Virginia Governor Benjamin Harrison and future Associate Justice of the US. Supreme Court John Blair, both graduates of the College of William & Mary.

In a breakthrough move, the board established America's first collegiate school of law in 1779 and named legal scholar and statesman George Wythe as its first Chair of Law and professor. This would become one of the most consequential events after July of 1776 in assuring the success of the new American experiment. Wythe followed England's legendary Sir William Blackstone as the second professor of common law in the English-speaking realm.

Harvard lays claim to having the oldest law school in America, with a proviso in small print: "in continuous operation." Harvard's program opened in 1817, fully thirty-eight years after William & Mary's law school in 1779. The Williamsburg program, however, closed for periods during the American Revolution, the Civil War, and times of economic hardship, to be revived in the early twentieth century.

At the time, Jefferson served as wartime governor of Virginia and was instrumental in Wythe's appointment. Their collaboration at the law school was among the first of several partnerships that would prove indispensable to the new nation.

Following his undergraduate training at the College of William & Mary, Jefferson had studied as Wythe's legal apprentice for five of his most formative years, beginning in his late teens. In addition to a comprehensive legal education, Jefferson under Wythe's tutelage was given the equivalent of an advanced degree in the humanities from one of the world's finest universities.

The young apprentice followed his mentor into Virginia's courtrooms and also into the colony's highest political circles. To Jefferson, fatherless at age fourteen, Wythe became not only his role model and surrogate father but also a lifelong friend. In turn, Wythe, having lost his only child in infancy, regarded Jefferson as a son.

At the time of his William & Mary appointment, Wythe was fifty-three and had already achieved status as senior statesman. His signature on the Declaration of Independence had been granted the top place of honor among those of his fellow Virginians, above that of Jefferson's. Of average height, he had an attractive countenance, a chiseled chin and a Roman nose, suitable for one of America's foremost Greek and Roman scholars.

He was known for his courtly bow, gracious manner, scholarship, and wry sense of humor. Unlike his wealthy friends, he dressed plainly and wore his brown hair naturally, without powdered wigs, reflecting his Quaker heritage. A large head framed his blue eyes and prominent features. His friends joked that his cranium needed to be big to house the huge amount of knowledge that he carried around.

Advisor to colonial governors and a member of Virginia's elite circles, Wythe was also a champion of the disenfranchised. Unlike those of his social class, he was an ardent opponent of slavery. As Virginia's High Court of Chancery judge, he ruled slavery illegal, based on the state's Declaration of Rights. The ruling was overturned by a higher court, but it was his stab at the entrenched institution. He lectured his William & Mary students on the wrongs of slavery, freed his own slaves when he was legally able to do so, and provided generously for several in his will.

The establishment of America's first collegiate law school was long overdue. Lawyers were held in such low regard during the first century of Virginia's settlement that they were banned entirely from the colony's courtrooms for eleven years, starting in 1646. This was only thirty-eight years after the first settlers arrived, followed not far behind by a trail of shysters from London.

In their wisdom, colonial leaders assumed that an honest man could be his best defender before a judge and jury of his peers, without interference by an unscrupulous barrister. The preamble to the legislation spoke to their concerns: "Many troublesome suits are multiplied by the unskillfulness and covetousness of attorneys, who have more intended their own profits and their inordinate lucre than the good and benefit of their clients."[4]

The Virginia legislature lifted the ban in 1657, replacing it with a system of fee regulation, oaths of office, and licensing. Lack of a law school and standardized qualifications for attorneys, however, created a kind of seat-of-the-pants justice in many colonial courtrooms. No law school would be founded in America for well over a hundred years. Most lawyers learned the trade as apprentices to senior attorneys, with uneven results.

George Wythe had begun his study of law as an apprentice, learning relatively little in the arrangement. As a second son, he had not been expected to inherit the family's farming property near Hampton, Virginia, and in his mid-teens, had to choose another means of earning a living.

After deciding to study law, he moved several counties away to apprentice under attorney Stephen Dewey, his mother's brother-in-law. Wythe's uncle proved too busy to bother with instruction and instead burdened the youth with reams of tedious paperwork for his law practice. Wythe, like many other apprentices, represented a convenient source of unpaid labor for a busy attorney.

Wythe soon realized that to become an educated man, he would need to teach himself. Subsequently, he began a lifetime learning journey, becoming one of America's finest self-taught scholars in law, government, the classics, languages, and the humanities. When the time came for him to teach jurisprudence to his students, he was determined to give his best.

Students enrolling in the new William & Mary Law School knew that their professor was not only a successful attorney but also a patriot of some renown. Known as a prophet of the American Revolution, he had been among the first to call for complete independence from England. He had taken time from his active law practice to serve in various public offices at local, state, and national levels.

Soon after his professorship appointment, Wythe taught his students the value of public service as well as the practice of law. With the collapse of English rule, hundreds of new positions were opening throughout America at all levels of government and in all levels of the court system. Filling these posts with qualified individuals would be a challenge.

During his years as teacher and mentor, Wythe educated nearly two hundred individuals, many who would shape the nascent nation's government and judiciary for future generations. At his death in 1806, his former students were virtually running the country. President Thomas Jefferson set America's national course. Chief Justice John Marshall and Justice Bushrod Washington weighed in on the Supreme Court, and John Breckinridge served as Attorney General. Rising political star Henry Clay and Buckner Thruston represented the important new state of Kentucky in the senate, joining William Branch Giles of Virginia. Spencer Roane of Virginia operated as one of the most influential judges in the nation.

William & Mary Law School graduates filled the legislature and courtrooms of Virginia as well as the nation's highest cabinet offices. By mentoring Jefferson in the ideals of statesmanship, Wythe also indirectly influenced the next two United States presidents from Virginia, Jefferson's younger protégés James Madison and James Monroe.

Counting his time as George Washington's personal attorney and legislative supporter, and as John Adams's friend and confidante in the Continental Congress, Wythe directly or indirectly influenced the country's first five presidents, who served for the first thirty-six seminal years of America's nationhood.

Wythe chose never to run for national office, but instead focused his attention on improving matters in Virginia, the largest and most influential state at the time. At the state and local level, his service included that of Chancellor of the Commonwealth of Virginia; Judge of Virginia's High Court of the Chancery; Virginia Attorney General; Delegate to the Continental Congress; Speaker of the Virginia House of Delegates; Clerk of the Virginia House of Burgesses; and Mayor of Williamsburg, the colonial capital.

Professor Wythe imparted to his William & Mary students a deep commitment to honorable conduct—that it would be better to cut off a hand than to dip it into the public till for personal gain. His reputation for integrity had grown over the years as attorney, judge, and legislator. He was the "only honest lawyer I ever knew," quipped a clergyman acquaintance.[5]

Wythe's honesty saved him from participating in what may have been one of America's first great political scandals. The incident rocked Virginia in 1766 after the death of John Robinson, influential speaker-treasurer of the House of Burgesses. Quietly and under the table in a complex money scheme, Robinson had given a number of his privileged, debt-ridden friends the equivalent of approximately one million dollars' worth of Virginia currency in what amounted to personal loans.

At the time, this was an enormous sum and represented a considerable breach of faith by the colony's leaders. In the legislature's disgrace, George Wythe stood as a notable exception. After that incident, Virginia lawmakers appointed him to an examining committee to review the state of the treasury twice a year.

More than a century after his death, the Virginia State Bar Association erected a plaque in Wythe's honor at the William & Mary Law School. It reads: "He was an exemplar of all that is noble and elevating in the profession of the law." The homage continues: "This tablet is erected in tribute to his courage as a patriot, his ability as an instructor, his uprightness as a lawyer, and his purity as a judge."

Among the individuals who could have been chosen to lead America's first law school, and subsequently its first leadership training program for future statesmen, Wythe proved indispensable.

Chapter Two
America's First
Leadership Training School

The purpose of higher education:

"To form the statesmen, legislators and judges, on
whom public prosperity and individual happiness
are so much to depend" [1]

—Thomas Jefferson, 1818

Among other Founding Fathers, Jefferson had
a healthy distrust of unethical individuals in power:
"Experience hath shown, that even under the best
forms of government those entrusted with power
have, in time, and by slow operations, perverted it
into tyranny." [2]

Founders of America's first, and for years only,
law school at the College of William & Mary fore-
saw that it could produce not only attorneys but
also future holders of the land's highest public and
judicial offices. American settlement was relatively
small then, only thirteen states, and one productive
school would have wide influence.

21

As noted, it was especially important to members of the college's new board of visitors that their law professor instill a high sense of ethics among the future leaders it produced. In a biographical sketch of Wythe, Jefferson observed: "No man ever left behind him a character more venerated than G. Wythe. His virtue was of the purest tint; his integrity inflexible, and his justice exact; of warm patriotism, and, devoted as he was to liberty, and to the natural and equal rights of man, he might truly be called the Cato of his country; for a more disinterested [fair minded] man never lived." [3]

Jefferson's reference to Cato was especially telling. Educated individuals at the time who studied Greek and Roman history and government would have understood the compliment. Marcus Portius Cato (95-46 BCE) was a patriot who fought tyranny to preserve government for the good of the people. A leader of the Roman Republic, he was a model of integrity, amid the self-dealing of others.

During his ten-year tenure at the William & Mary Law School between 1779 and 1789, Wythe became a rock-star professor. The brightest and best students of the region traveled to Williamsburg for studies in law and the humanities. No one was prouder of Wythe's accomplishments than his surrogate son, Jefferson.

Jefferson's friend Ralph Izard wrote to him in 1788 asking for advice about where to send his son to college. Recommending William & Mary, Jefferson replied: "I know of no place in the world, while the present professors remain, where I would so soon place a son."

He continued: "The pride of the Institution is Mr. Wythe, one of the Chancellors of the State, and Professor of Law in the College. He is one of the greatest men of the age, having held without competition the first place at the Bar of our General Court for 25 years, and always distinguished by the most spotless virtue." [4]

Wythe's student legacy includes a noteworthy number of offices: a United States president and vice president, a Supreme Court chief justice and associate justice, five secretaries of state, two attorneys general, seven state governors, and numerous high-ranking congressmen, senators, cabinet officers, judges, and legislators in multiple states.

Like a large stone thrown into a small pond, the influence of the William & Mary Law School and its first professor had a ripple effect, spreading widely with the expansion of America. Wythe's students carried his teachings westward into Kentucky and beyond, founding the first law school west of the mountains. During the nineteenth century, Transylvania University in Kentucky graduated a remarkable number of senators, congressmen, cabinet officers, governors, judges, foreign diplomats, and other eminent officials.

Reviewing William & Mary's legacy, twentieth century Law School Dean Oscar Shewmake observed:

> *No law school in America has since sent from its classrooms into public life, in the same length of time, if at all, an equal number of men of such amazing ability. Within a surprisingly short time his students [assumed] positions of high responsibility in such numbers that it is perhaps not going too far to say that the mind of George Wythe, acting through those whom he had taught, dominated the policies of this republic for fully fifty years, and is still a potent force."* [5]

Students were attracted to the new law school in part due to the professor's reputation as one of the Revolution's important patriots. In addition to signing the Declaration of Independence, Wythe

helped organize its second section, the list of griev-
ances against King George III. Through letters to
the governors of colonies, he sought documentation of English atrocities, understanding as an experienced attorney that the Declaration was to be
fledgling America's legal brief before the court of
world opinion.

By also mentoring Jefferson in the Enlightenment philosophy reflected in Jefferson's noble preamble, Wythe earned the designation "Godfather
of the Declaration of Independence" by the late
United States Supreme Court Justice Lewis F. Powell, Jr., a fellow Virginian.[6] Wythe also worked on a
committee that wrote a precursor to the Declaration, an "animated address," days before Jefferson
began his writing. Jefferson carefully studied the
document, in Wythe's handwriting, before completing his draft.

In the months leading up to independence, as
General Washington prepared for battle with England, Wythe and his friend John Adams were
among the workhorses of the Continental Congress, commissioning supplies, raising funds, and
exhorting others to support the Revolution

As hostilities mounted, Wythe called for a navy,
worked to enlist allies, and endangered his life by

openly criticizing the King. Later, his house in Williamsburg served as campaign headquarters for American and French military officers before and after the Battle of Yorktown.

Clearly, Wythe had committed treason against British authority. Hanging was the most humane treatment for treason, with drawing and quartering the most draconian. In any case, he made himself a marked man. He remained so when he took the public job of college professor in Williamsburg during the height of warfare with England, two years before the truce at Yorktown.

A room in the historic Wren Building on the college grounds served as the law school's classroom. Built eight decades earlier at the end of the seventeenth century, the stately mellow brick structure had already withstood the first of its three disastrous fires and would ultimately become the oldest college building still standing in the United States. Known simply as "The College," it was renamed later for English architect Sir Christopher Wren, said to have provided the basis for the original design.

Before the installation of central heat and air conditioning in modern times, students and teachers endured extremes of heat and cold in the old structure as seasons changed. Fireplaces provided only minimal comfort in January. Hot months covered Tidewater Virginia in a humid blanket that permeated every inch of a man's formal wool and cotton clothing. Open windows carried the smell of manure and urine from hundreds of horses, cattle, sheep, and hogs trudging the streets and housed in backyard barns. Horseflies, straight from miles of dung heaps, plagued human necks and faces.

Yet, students flocked to the building for their legal training, used to such eighteenth- century discomforts. Many entering the school would have been content with receiving only a course in law— and then departing quickly to make a good living. But Wythe wanted to impart more to them than the practice of a profession.

He insisted that they become thoroughly well-informed individuals and gave them an education in history, government, philosophy, debate, the heritage of ancient Greece and Rome, and a host of other subjects. He further encouraged them to become dedicated public servants with a strong sense of ethics.

In class, Wythe refined the Socratic method of teaching, holding student interest through a line of questioning rather than delivering a tedious recital

27

of facts. He also believed in learning by doing, his teaching techniques presaging modern educational methods. To train his future lawyers and statesmen, he turned Virginia's old Capitol Building into a lively theater of sorts, for his students to perform and shine before an appreciative audience of town folk. Wearing their Sunday best, future lawyers debated cases in moot courts. Future statesmen proposed and argued laws in mock legislatures, learning from each other's mistakes as well as from their talents. Reviving the moot court tradition from London's medieval Inns of Court, Wythe embraced this kind of forensic training for his students. Similar teaching techniques, combining theory and practice, were later adopted by Harvard and other American universities.

Future lawyers were assigned cases to prepare and debate before an audience. Professors from the college served as judges. The atmosphere was similar to regular court days, when local folk gathered for entertainment and information. In mock legislative sessions, Wythe trained his students in statecraft. As a classical scholar, he knew that ancient Athenians loved debate—that they incorporated the practice of public discourse into their governing process. Wythe studied and applied this model.

As Virginia's former Speaker of the House, the professor was uniquely qualified to preside over the debates, sitting in the large high-back chair, or "throne," that he had used during legislative sessions. He taught his students parliamentary procedure and supervised as they formed committees, drew up bills, and then presented, debated, and revised the bills.

These popular sessions were held on Saturdays when local residents could fill the wooden seats to see the show. Young women in the crowd followed marriageable young men as they prepared for promising careers; a degree from the William & Mary Law School was a ticket to professional and social success. Considered eligible for marriage at sixteen and eighteen, they hoped to see some of the students in the evening at one of Williamsburg's numerous soirees. The town offered an active social life in its heyday before Virginia's capital moved to Richmond.

William & Mary's Law School attracted students from throughout Virginia and the mid-Atlantic region. In its mock legislature, future lawmakers from new western mountain valley towns deliberated with sons from established, wealthy Tidewater planter families. The student

body included city boys and country boys, tradi-
tionalists and progressives.

It is likely that Professor Wythe asked his
pupils to consider several of his own proposed laws
from his 1777-1779 committee work in revising Virginia's legal code. Some of the revision's greatest
reform measures were languishing in Virginia's legislature. Among them was a groundbreaking act for
religious freedom, resulting from Wythe's collaboration with Thomas Jefferson, who wrote the final
draft. This law would linger at the Virginia General
Assembly until 1786 and would eventually become
incorporated in the First Amendment to the Constitution. Likewise, the Jefferson-Wythe proposals
for universal public education in Virginia went virtually ignored for decades.

Students debating such proposed laws in the
mock legislature were often acting more expedi-
tiously on important reforms than their elders in
the real legislature. "Some of their harangues wou'd
be heard with pleasure in any house of representatives," Walker Maury wrote to Thomas Jefferson in
1784, reporting that debates were conducted with
"more spirit than was ever dispay'd in any institution of this nature." He added, "As to the university,
I cannot conceive an institution better planned, or

more judiciously managed for the forming, either the lawyer, or the statesman."

With a nod to Jefferson's legal training, Maury noted: "You can judge better than I can, what advantages youth must reap from meeting twice a week in Mr. Wythe's school, and going thro all the forms of pleadings of a court of judicature, with the utmost exactness and decorum, and from assembling once a fortnight, as a body of Legislators, in whom you see our assembly in miniature debating, at least many of them, extempore, on important questions of state. . . . Mr. Wythe indeed seems to enjoy himself no where, so much as with his pupils." [7]

The Wikipedia biographer of Christopher Columbus Langdell, dean of the Harvard Law School in the late-nineteenth century, credits Langdell with inventing the "case study" method of legal training, but it was Wythe decades earlier who broke ground with his moot courts using sample cases, mock legislatures where bills were debated, and revival of the Socratic method of instruction. The Wikipedia post calls Langdell "arguably the most influential teacher of professional education in the United States." Students of George Wythe's career and student achievement may wish to argue the point.

As word spread about the law school's Saturday performances, the number of spectators grew. One student noted that the day of his "political birth" was the Saturday he "delivered an oration for the first time." Another student, John Brown, wrote that he took an active part in training sessions, hoping they would relieve him of some of his extreme bashfulness, while enjoying welcome relief from the harder studies. Brown later became a successful United States senator from Kentucky. [8]

Another student, Thomas Lee Shippen, wrote to his parents: "Last Saturday was the day of my political birth, if I may call so, the day on which I first assumed the character of a Legislator: for then I delivered an oration for the first time in our grand and august Assembly." Shippen wrote about being intimidated by Professor Wythe sitting in his lofty seat, presiding over and evaluating his students' presentations: "I was prodigiously alarmed to be sure."

At the end, he was rewarded for his hard work. "I surmounted the difficulties which were opposed to me by my diffidence, my youth, and the solemnity of the occasion, much better than I myself or any of my friends expected: And the applause I met with tho I did not think I deserved it, repaid me for the pain and anxiety I felt on the occasion." Shippen unfortunately died before he realized his full potential. It would have been interesting to see how he might have taken his place among the stars in the law school's constellation of leaders. [9]

The professor gave much to his students, and he demanded much in return. He spread before them a vast field of knowledge and expected them to avail themselves of it. Wythe continually added to his store of books, and his collection of more than five hundred volumes was one of the most important libraries in eighteenth-century America.

For the study of law, he provided books on Roman, English, and American law, property, equity, administrative, civil, commercial, criminal, contract, ecclesiastical, and constitutional law. There were volumes of case reports, digests, statutes, and legal treatises. To round out his students' educations, he purchased books on government, ancient and modern history, mathematics, engineering, astronomy, art, philosophy, religion, science, medicine, language, and rhetoric. His array of literature included English, French, Greek, Latin, Scottish, Spanish, and American.

For the best students, the results of such an education were spectacular. "After being buried for five or six years," Wythe protégé William Munford reported, "we see them [Wythe's students] merge from their hiding places and shine forth with a splendor that dazzles the continent." He wrote to his friend John Coalter that he looked forward to studying law under Wythe with "pleasure and alacrity." He surmised that "even my improvement is not to be doubted," given Wythe's "attentions and willingness to inform." [10]

John Coalter was equally pleased to have been accepted into the law school. He wrote to his father: "I have just begun to attend Mr. Wythe on Law. . . .the exalted character and tried abilities of that Gentleman promise the apt and diligent student a certain and noble source of instruction." Coalter later became a well-regarded judge on the Supreme Court of Virginia. [11]

At the William & Mary Law School, the ideal of the Citizen Lawyer was carried down through succeeding generations of students. Defined as working ethically and unselfishly for the public good, the concept of servant leadership was first articulated by classical thinkers like Plato, Aristotle, Cicero, and others of their philosophy. While he did not originate the concept, Wythe can be given credit for helping to revive the ideal as a driv-ing force among early American leaders.

The early principles established in the law school are sometimes referred to today nostalgi-cally as the Virginia Way. Viewed in an idealistic light, the Virginia Way embodied the tradition of civility and integrity in public service. It was the antithesis of shouting matches, winner-take-all par-tisan politics, self-dealing, and government by spe-cial interests. Lawmakers, judges, and other officials were expected to serve the public with honor. For generations, Virginia largely escaped the govern-ment corruption that erupted in the nineteenth century in places like New York and Boston.

By all accounts, Wythe's students revered him. Many, including Thomas Jefferson and Henry Clay, named a son or grandson after him. Biographer Dice Robins Anderson described what he believed Wythe brought to his classroom: scholarship, inge-nuity of method, genuine love of subject, and "most important off all, a deep affection for the young men who ate of the bread of life which he broke."

Wythe's students were to him "not receptacles, not apparatus, not material for experimentation, not means of livelihood; they were living souls, they were generous hearted friends, they were companions journeying with him along the road to truth and manliness."[12] Years later, historian David Mc-Cullough would underscore the point: "Teachers are the most important people in our society."[13]

Wythe was mindful that members of the Founding Fathers' "greatest generation" were aging. It became an imperative to train the next cohort of leaders. His friend John Adams shared his concerns about the caliber of individuals who could assume leadership in the new government. At the time of the Constitution's ratification, Adams wrote: "Public business must always be done by somebody. It will be done by somebody or another. If wise men decline it, others will not; if honest men refuse it, others will not."[14]

Wythe's goal was clear. In 1783, at the height of his college teaching career, he wrote to Adams that his objective was to "form such characters as may be fit to succeed those which have been ornamental and useful in the national council of America." [15]

Adams had encouraged Wythe in this regard in a letter in April of 1776. The two had formed a close bond as delegates in the 1775-76 Second Continental Congress in Philadelphia. The letter, titled "Thoughts on Government," is considered among Adams's most important papers. In this message to

Wythe, he outlines the need for a constitution, three branches of government, two houses of Congress, and the future structure of the nation's judiciary. He clearly saw the pitfalls of an all-powerful government with few checks and balances.

In 1776, Adams could scarcely contain his optimism about what lay ahead for America as a free nation, capable of charting its own independent course:

> *You and I, my dear friend, have been sent into life at a time when the greatest lawgivers of antiquity would have wished to live. How few of the human race have ever enjoyed an opportunity of making an election of government, more than of air, soil, or climate, for themselves or their children! When, before the present epocha, had three millions of people full power and a fair opportunity to form and establish the wisest and happiest government that human wisdom can contrive? I hope you will avail yourself and your country of that extensive learning and indefatigable industry which you possess, to assist her in the formation of the happiest governments and the best character of a great people.[16]*

Despite such enthusiasm about the future, Adams's wife, Abigail, also worried about the possibilities of America's government falling to unethical leaders. Considered her husband's intellectual equal, she was a prolific, ceaseless letter writer. An astute observer of human behavior, she understood the ambitions of politicians.

She wrote, "All men would be tyrants if they could." Of ego-centrists, she noted: "How difficult the task to quench the fire and the pride of private ambition, and to sacrifice ourselves and all our hopes and expectations to the public weal! How few have souls capable of so noble an undertaking!" Observing a nascent nation in turmoil during and after the Revolution, she declared, "Great necessities call out great virtues" and "I am interested in power that is moral, that is right, and that is good."[17]

As few of Wythe's letters have survived, it is not known whether there was any correspondence between Abigail Adams and George Wythe. She would have known, however, about her husband's regard for the professor.

William & Mary's Law School opened during some of the most difficult days of the Revolution. Many students had left class to become warriors.

The school closed for eighteen months during the conflict, the college and town having become an armed camp.

In 1781, British troops invaded Williamsburg, eating everything in sight and looting houses and stores. It seemed as if a plague had descended on the city—vicious enemy soldiers marauding through homes, an outbreak of smallpox, and swarms of biting black flies. Even worse, one of the town's occupiers was America's foremost traitor, Benedict Arnold.

In the early fall of 1781, English troops planned for battle at nearby Yorktown. In mid-September, George Washington rode into Williamsburg, and Wythe offered his home to the general and his staff. Washington, tall and erect on his warhorse, cut a striking figure in full-dress uniform as he passed by the waving and cheering town folk.

Wythe and Washington were long-time friends, beginning with their service as young men in the Virginia House of Burgesses. Wythe was Washington's personal lawyer and supported him in both the French and Indian War and the American Revolution, in behind-the-scenes legislative funding, first in the Virginia House of Burgesses and later in the Continental Congress.

Wythe's dignified brick manor house on Palace Green served as Washington's strategic planning headquarters for the conflict ahead. He transformed the elegant dining area into a war room, strewn with maps of tactical terrain. The general's battle-hardened staff found temporary respite in the comfortable upstairs bedrooms.

After victory at Yorktown, achieved with crucial support from France, French General Compe de Rochambeau moved into the home, raising a toast in triumph. Numerous French soldiers, however, had been maimed and killed in the conflict. At the beginning of battle, French officers had taken over the Wren building at the college where law school classes had been conducted.

For nine months, the venerable structure was used as a military hospital for wounded and dying soldiers. It was a gory scene. Doctors amputated legs and arms with saws and stacked them for disposal. Crimson stains bled into the old brown wooden floors of the law school, and soldiers screamed in pain in their native tongue, to little relief. French soldiers were foreigners sent to free a foreign land. Their country's own fight for liberation from kings and aristocracy was yet to come.

When not in battle, some French leaders took

the time to admire the ambiance of the old college. General Francois-Jean de Chastellux wrote: "The beauty of the building is surpassed by the richness of its library, and still farther by the distinguished merit of . . . its professors, such as the Doctors Madison, Wythe, Bellini . . . who may be regarded as living Books." He added that these professors "have already formed many distinguished characters, ready to serve their country in the various departments of government." [18]

Although Wythe understood the necessity of accommodating America's French allies, he had a gnawing fear that his precious library and expensive scientific instruments were in jeopardy in the college building. Understanding that General Washington had larger worries on his mind, Wythe nevertheless took time to write his concerns to his friend on October 25, 1781. Wythe had reason for alarm. In the wreckage of war, the Wren building, the college president's house, and several outbuildings were damaged, and Wythe's prized library burned in flames.

Like many of the Founding Fathers, Wythe was left much poorer by the war. He had inherited his family's farm at the death of his older brother and had relied on its income to supplement the low salary he received as college professor. His agricultural operations had been devastated by his Loyalist farm manager's collaborations with the English military and by other depredations.

Hoping to resume teaching as soon as possible, Wythe urged wartime officers to free William & Mary's classrooms as soon as the hospital could be moved elsewhere. He wrote a letter to Thomas Jefferson on December 31 about his concerns. It would be five more months before the French left in May, 1782, and many months afterward before the buildings could be fully repaired. To the French government's credit, two years later it paid to rebuild the college president's house. In 1786, perhaps at the suggestion of Thomas Jefferson, then American ambassador to France, King Louis XVI gave two hundred books to the college library in additional compensation.

After the war, young veterans of the Revolution, some wounded from battle, returned to educations interrupted by the conflict. Wythe's good friend, Richard Henry Lee, from one of Virginia's prominent families, wrote in February of 1783 about a son who had been studying in England: "My son Ludwell comes again to put himself under your patronage in his Law studies, from whence we both regretted that he was compelled to remove by the necessities of the times."

Lee said that independent of his friendship with Wythe, he believed strongly in encouraging Virginia's youth to pursue their studies under the good professor rather than travel elsewhere. "I understand that young gentlemen now of Philadelphia propose to finish their studies with you. My son will in all things follow your friendly advice and be grateful to the bestower for giving it." He ended by congratulating Wythe for his part in winning America's independence and the "general peace that has already taken place." [19]

It is said that there were two American revolutions—one fought on the battlefield and another in legislative assemblies, as representatives attempted to create an entirely new form of government. Like many eighteenth-century intellectuals, Wythe believed in an ordered universe—laws of nature governed the natural world, and just laws should govern the human world. Laws passed by elected officials and adjudicated by judges should therefore be mankind's best expression of modeling an orderly society, for the benefit of everyone in that society.

Unfortunately, Wythe's correspondence on matters of importance, as well as his college lecture papers, have not survived. Most of what we know about him consists of the facts of his life and what others said of him. Had his writings been preserved, he would be better known as one of America's most consequential Founding Fathers. Possibly, the lack of surviving paperwork is due to Wythe's having no descendants to carry on his legacy. Those who removed or destroyed his letters and lecture notes likely had little idea of their historic value.

Brief biographical sketches survive. He was born on his family's plantation, Chesterville, in the Hampton, Virginia area, in 1726, fifty years before signing the Declaration of Independence. NASA's Langley Research Center is located on the homeplace. A student of astronomy, he would have been intrigued by its trailblazing work in space.

The Wythes were a long-established family in Virginia's Tidewater region, dating to 1680 when Wythe's great-grandfather, Thomas Wythe senior, emigrated from Norfolk, England. Men in the family quickly took their places as Virginia legislators and magistrates. George Wythe's maverick streak, however, probably reflected his mother's Quaker heritage—a belief in the equality of individuals, freedom of thought, justice, humility, and an antipathy toward slavery.

Among the few educated women in the region, Margaret Wythe was said to have taught her son Latin and Greek, setting him on a lifetime journey of scholarship. She became his primary mentor at age three after the early death of his father, Thomas. Wythe spent his middle years in Williamsburg as attorney, legislator, and college professor. Upon assuming heavy responsibilities as judge of Virginia's High Court of the Chancery, he moved to the new state capital, Richmond, for his last fifteen years.

He was married and widowed twice. While practicing law in his early twenties in Fredericksburg, Virginia, he fell in love with his law partner's daughter, Ann Lewis. She died after only eight months of marriage of unknown causes, perhaps from complications of pregnancy or in one of the frequent fever epidemics that plagued the colony. Life expectancy for colonial women was relentlessly short.

Grieving the loss, Wythe left for Williamsburg and remained single for seven years until marrying Elizabeth Taliaferro in 1755. Her father, well-known builder and planter Richard Taliaferro, gave the couple their manor house on Palace Green for life tenancy as a wedding present. They were married for more than thirty years with no surviving children. Less than a year after Wythe's death in 1806, a Wythe biographer for the *American Gleaner and Virginia Magazine*, hopeful then that Wythe's name would be honored in history, nevertheless foreshadowed Wythe's eventual status as Forgotten Founding Father: "The fame of the disturbers and destroyers of mankind is generally sounded very loudly by poets and historians, while the names of the peaceful benefactors of their species, of those who were noted only for virtue and wisdom, are often suffered silently to sink into oblivion."[20]

A little more than a hundred years later, in December of 1921, students in the law school that Wythe founded at the College of William & Mary had scant knowledge of the man. After an interruption of sixty years beginning with the Civil War, Dean Oscar L Shewmake revived the historic school in 1921-1922 under the name "Marshall-Wythe School of Law" that later returned to its more easily recognizable "William & Mary Law School."

"The world knows little of its greatest men," noted Shewmake, quoting English writer Sir Henry Taylor, in an address before the college's Wythe Law Club. He began his biographical sketch of Wythe with the words: "Fame, in the common acceptation of the word, is a fleeting thing."

He then reminded young William & Mary law students in the audience that the world regards as its truly great men those whose personal integrity, intellectual honesty, moral courage, and unselfish devotion to duty provide examples to be followed long after the events of their lives are forgotten. [21]

Chapter Three
Leading Under the Constitution

The happy Union of these States is a wonder;
their Constitution a miracle;
their example the hope of Liberty
throughout the world. [1]
—James Madison, 1829

William & Mary Law School students were the first in the nation to study constitutional law. Further, William & Mary Law School graduates, under the influence of their former professor, were instrumental in saving the United States Constitution from failure during its critical ratification round in Virginia.

Today, it is hard to imagine a nation filled with lawyers and judges, and not one trained in its founding document. Yet, that was the case in 1789, when the Constitution became the law of the land, fully thirteen years after America declared independence.

Article VI of the Constitution specifies duties for judges and legislators: ". . . . the judges in every state shall be bound thereby, anything in the Constitution or laws of any State to the contrary notwithstanding. The Senators and Representatives before mentioned, and the members of the several state legislatures, and all executive and judicial officers, both of the United States and of the several states, shall be bound by oath or affirmation, to support this Constitution."

At the time of the Constitution's ratification and for years later, the College of William & Mary served as the only law school in the country, and its graduates would be the nation's only judges and attorneys trained in constitutional law at the university level. Others would be trusted to study the founding document on their own.

A champion of the Constitution, Wythe would have introduced the document during his last year at the law school. His successor at the college, St. George Tucker, extended Wythe's teaching philosophy for another fifteen years. One of Wythe's star pupils and later his own personal attorney, Tucker assumed the professorship in Williamsburg in 1789, after Wythe's resignation to attend to duties in Richmond as judge of the High Court of Chancery of Virginia.

Between 1789 and 1804, Tucker lectured on standard English law texts, while instructing his students that federal and state laws passed by American legislators were more important than simply learning about English common law. Harvard's law school would not open for another thirteen years after the end of Tucker's tenure, followed a year later by Jefferson's law school at the University of Virginia.

Young Henry Clay, who later became one of America's most consequential statesmen, was taught to honor the Constitution during his private education under George Wythe and Virginia Attorney General Robert Brooke in the 1790's. Later, he taught constitutional law at the law school that he and other former Wythe students founded in Kentucky. He wrote: "The Constitution of the United States was made not merely for the generation that then existed, but for posterity—unlimited, undefined, endless, perpetual posterity." [2]

Although many of Wythe's former pupils would adjudicate constitutional law, no one did so as powerfully as United States Supreme Court Chief Justice John Marshall. As the longest serving and one of America's most influential chief justices, he strengthened the nation's understanding of constitutional law in many of the one thousand decisions issued by his court during his tenure from 1801 to

1835. His interpretation of the Constitution elevated the authority of the Supreme Court as an equal branch of government, one whose decisions were final.

Few today realize how close the Constitution came to failure during its ratification rounds. In some states, it survived by a margin of fewer than five votes. Virginia's vote in 1788 was pivotal, and the role of William & Mary's Professor Wythe and William & Mary graduates is especially noteworthy.

The year earlier, Wythe had been chosen for a key leadership role in the national Constitutional Convention in Philadelphia, convening in May of 1787. After disbanding classes for the summer, he traveled to Pennsylvania at his own expense, as he had done a dozen years earlier to serve in the Continental Congress at the beginning of the Revolution.

Delegates to the convention were far from united concerning the nation's future government. The weather was hot, as were tempers on occasion. Doors of the State House were closed to protect confidentiality. Without a strong sense of order and purpose, leaders sensed that the convention could fall apart. Rules of conduct were necessary, and Wythe, known as an authority on parliamentary procedure and government, was chosen to direct the writing of rules to govern the convention.

Some of the rules were similar to the simple good etiquette he expected of his students back at the College of William & Mary—for example, not to read books, pamphlets, or any other printed materials during active sessions of the assembly. (In a later age, the instruction would be to silence all cellphones and refrain from texting while others speak.) It was specified that no man could leave the convention unless his state remained fully represented without him.

Rules were set for quorums, voting, amendments, and reconsideration. Free discussion was allowed, and delegates could return to subjects that had already been deliberated. All proceedings would be kept absolutely secret. Without Wythe's sensible procedures, the convention could have become mired in its own confusion. Three days after the group met, Wythe reported the rules of procedure, and members of the convention adopted them virtually unchanged.

Few recognized the importance of the convention's work more than George Wythe. Normally, he likely would have engaged in the proceedings for several months until approval of the final document in September. Hearing of the worsening health of his wife Elizabeth in Williamsburg, however, he made a decision to leave Philadelphia on June 4, 1787, to stay at her bedside. She died in August, from a lingering illness.

One year later, in June of 1788, the fate of the Constitution would be in question during Virginia's critical Ratifying Convention. All eyes were on the state: wealthy, large, and prominent, its borders then reaching all the way to the Mississippi River. As home to some of America's most important frontrunners—Washington, Jefferson, Madison, Monroe, Mason and Wythe—Virginia was a recognized thought-leader.

Although the required number of nine states had already ratified the Constitution, Virginia played a critical role in having it supported by all thirteen states, binding the former colonies together as the United States of America.

"Anti-rats" and "pro-rats" from throughout Virginia descended upon Richmond to argue the ratification vote. Virginia had been slow to ratify. Among the thirteen new states, it would be the tenth to confirm. Leaders in New York, North Carolina and Rhode Island were watching Virginia before casting their votes.

Powerful states-rights forces lined up against Virginia's ratification, led by Patrick Henry. He took the floor for hours at a time, attempting to sway indecisive voters with urgent oratory that previewed the modern political filibuster. As large as some European nations, Virginia prided its independence and feared an over-reaching national government. Among other reservations, Henry's contingent was wary of a powerful authority that could eventually outlaw slavery, a system upon which most of Virginia's wealth depended. Henry summed up his views on the ratifying argument: "I smelt a rat."[3]

James Madison, known as the Father of the Constitution, argued eloquently on the Constitution's behalf. But at age thirty-seven, he was among the younger Founding Fathers. It took the authority of senior statesman George Wythe, sixty-two, to sway the crowd in the final round.

Former William & Mary Law School Dean Oscar Shewmake defined his influence: "But for Wythe's services in the Convention of 1788, Virginia would not have ratified the Constitution of the United States as it stood. . .The entire course of American history may have been materially changed." [4]

On June 4, the convention structured itself into a format that would allow for full debate on the Constitution. Wythe's colleagues unanimously made him chairman of the Committee of the Whole in view of his organization skills and knowledge of parliamentary procedure.

It must have been satisfying for Professor Wythe, nearing the end of his teaching career at William & Mary, to see many of his former law students as he looked out over the leaders assembled for the convention. This was an impressive gathering of one hundred seventy of the state's foremost citizens—older men who had fought in the Revolution and created the new state of Virginia and young men who would be its future leaders. Missing were Thomas Jefferson, in France, and future president George Washington, who favored the Constitution but wanted to stay above Virginia's political fray.

For nearly four contentious weeks, debate flared. As chairman of the Committee of the Whole, it was Wythe's job to listen to others debate and to move things along through proper parliamentary procedure. An impressive group lined up on the opposing side, including Patrick Henry, James Monroe, George Mason, Benjamin Harrison,

John Tyler Sr., Harry Innes, and William Grayson. The convention would be a clash of titans—Virginia's most powerful men pitted against one other in a fight for the future of their state and nation.

Supported by independent small farmers and those from the Kentucky region, anti-Federalists feared an all-powerful national government. They wanted amendments to guarantee personal liberties and to temper central control. Rumors flew about a monstrous federal authority that would invade private homes, stifle free speech, drown the citizens in unfair taxes, and usher in a new reign of tyranny.

Former William & Mary law student, thirty-three-year-old John Marshall, took the floor on June 10 to assure anti-ratification politicians that approving the new governing document was in the best interests of Virginia and the nation. He declared: "The supporters of the Constitution claim the title of being firm friends of the liberty and the rights of mankind. They say that they consider it as the best means of protecting liberty. . . . Let us try it and keep our hands free to change it when necessary." [5]

Patrick Henry, who helped ignite the Revolution with his oratory, devoted every rhetorical skill within his power to persuade his fellow Virginians to vote against the Constitution's ratification. A five-time governor of Virginia, immortalized for his "Give me liberty, or give me death" speech before the war, he was a commanding presence with a strong following.

From his chair as presiding officer, Wythe watched Henry perform before the audience. He still harbored some of the same reservations about Henry's edification that had given him pause years before while evaluating Henry's qualifications for a law license. Henry had walked into the convention full of sound and fury, often giving three speeches a day, haranguing the delegates. He delivered eight orations one day and five another, sometimes speaking as long as seven hours at a time. Debate was often negative and personal.

On June 24, Wythe asked Thomas Mathews to chair the meeting so that Wythe could address the group for the first time. He had saved his gunpowder for the end of battle. Delegates stopped their chatter to listen. Every face was turned toward the senior statesman, a living legend.

By this time in the acidic debate, Wythe's face had become drawn and pale and his voice low, choked with emotion. He recalled America's hard-won freedom from England. One by one, he outlined weaknesses of the present loose confederation of states. The country's initial Articles of Confederation were drafted and approved in the heat of war. They served a purpose then, but now were troublesome and inadequate for America's strong future. Without the unifying strength of a national Constitution, the United States of America could falter. Wythe agreed that the Constitution was not perfect, but he challenged its opponents to deny its excellent parts. He did not deny that amendments might be needed.

Wythe's method of operating was to avoid vitriol and partisanship and to present instead a way forward. While pointing out deficiencies in the existing system, Wythe fixed the assembly's thoughts on a more positive future for America, attempting to elevate the discourse. He stressed that a firm, indissoluble union of the states could further freedom, happiness, and independence for all of the citizenry.

Eventually Wythe, together with several other influential men, managed to outmaneuver ratification opponents by presenting a compromise that could be approved by a small but sufficient majority of delegates present. Wythe chaired a committee that drafted a resolution asserting that the central government would have only the powers delegated to it and that these could be revoked whenever they oppressed the people. He broke the stalemate with the compromise: If Virginia's delegates approved the Constitution, understanding that it had certain flaws, they could write proposed amendments for future adoption by the United States Congress.

The first ten amendments essentially became America's Bill of Rights, authored by James Madison, adopted by Congress in 1789, and ratified in 1791 by all of the states. But ratification of the Constitution had to come first. Wythe presented the resolution for ratification to Virginia delegates, again reminding them that amendments preserving individual and states' rights would follow. Patrick Henry wanted to filibuster again, have the last say, and extend the debate. But delegates were tired and hot, ready for the talk to end.

By a narrow margin of only ten votes, eighty-nine to seventy-nine, the convention voted to ratify the Constitution of the United States on June 25, 1788. If Virginia had been considered an indispensable player in the successful ratification of the United States Constitution, it could be argued that William & Mary graduates were indispensable to its successful passage in that key state. They provided well over the required number of affirmative votes.

Graduates of the William & Mary Law School voting in the affirmative included John Marshall, Archibald Stuart, James Innes, George Nicholas, Wilson Cary Nicholas, John Roane, Bushrod Washington, and also Virginia Governor Edmund Randolph, said to have been tutored privately by Wythe, or otherwise under his strong influence.

Those voting to ratify who had attended the college as undergraduates included the influential Edmund Pendleton, president of the Virginia Ratifying Convention, John Allen, John Blair Jr., Nathaniel Burwell, William Overton Callis, Littleton Eyre, Walter Jones, and David Stuart. Others voting in the affirmative were Robert Andrews, who served on the College of William & Mary faculty, and Francis Corbin, a member of the board of visitors. Corbin became rector in 1790.

Thomas Jefferson, though absent in France, supported Virginia's ratification. He wrote to Madison in March of 1789 that the Bill of Rights would be an effective check on government's abuse of power when these laws were in the hands of judges such as George Wythe. Madison, whom history recognizes as the shepherd of the Constitu-

tion, gave Wythe and his colleagues his personal
thanks for their work.[6]

New York, North Carolina, and Rhode Island
followed Virginia's lead. Two of their decisions to
ratify were exceedingly narrow: New York by only
three votes and Rhode Island by just two. The
Constitution of the United States prevailed. It has
survived as the world's oldest written constitution,
a model for countries on every continent.

Chapter Four
Educating Judges

"The dignity and stability of government
in all its branches, the morals of the people
and every blessing of society depend so much
upon an upright and skillful
administration of justice." [1]

—John Adams

In addition to Supreme Court Chief Justice John Marshall, the William & Mary Law School trained numerous other influential judges at the national and state level during its first decade. For those responsible for appointing judges to the bench, judicial integrity was a fundamental requirement.

John Adams, along with William & Mary Law School founders and other leaders, understood that the young nation would not be successful without a well-functioning court system. Legislators could pass laws, but these laws needed to be adjudicated skillfully and ethically.

Unprincipled judges could undermine America's great experiment as a democratic republic.

Bribery was a way of life throughout the world then, as it is now in many nations. The corruption of judges is as old as the court system itself.

Ancient Greek and Roman philosophers weighed in on the subject. Horace: "A corrupt judge is not qualified to inquire into the truth. A good and faithful judge ever prefers the honorable to the expedient." Sophocles: "How dreadful it is when the right judge judges wrong."

Old Russian proverbs are replete with references: "Tell God the truth, but give the judge money." "A golden handshake convinces even the most skeptical judge." "Law is like the shaft of a cart, it points wherever you turn it to." "Law is a flag, and gold is the wind that makes it wave." And: "If the pocket is empty, the judge is deaf."

As both had practiced law in Virginia's courtrooms and Wythe was long experienced as a judge, Jefferson and Wythe knew the pitfalls. Prior to the opening of the Williamsburg law school, aspiring attorneys and judges had basically two options to learn the law: costly travel to London to study at the Inns of Court, or a less expensive apprenticeship with a senior attorney. Few colonists could afford the option of studying in England; apprenticeship education stateside often proved to be uneven and of poor quality.

The problem of unqualified attorneys and judges was national in scope, not just a concern for Virginians. Only wealthy families could afford to send their sons to London for a scholarly education. There they were schooled in English law, not in the new laws being written in the emerging nation across the Atlantic. At the outbreak of war, many London-trained lawyers in America either fled to England or remained loyal to the Crown, losing respect among patriots.

The vast majority of future lawyers and judges in America received their initial lessons in the law as apprentices to senior attorneys. Their training was only as good as that of their teachers, and their lessons were given only as often as their mentors chose to provide them. Many apprentices, such as George Wythe, labored mostly in dusty rooms transcribing writs, a form of free labor.

Through hard work and self-study over a lifetime, Wythe earned distinction as the Father of American Jurisprudence.[2] He spent more than sixty years in the legal profession on both sides of the bench. He loved the law, studied law, practiced law, wrote laws, taught law, and adjudicated laws. His studies ranged from ancient Greek and Roman practices to Blackstone's ponderous *Commentaries on the Laws of England.*

Wythe's judicial career included service as a county magistrate, Attorney General of the Colony of Virginia, first Chancellor of the Commonwealth of Virginia, and inaugural holder of the judgeship of Virginia's High Court of Chancery. He served as a state judge while teaching law during his last year at William & Mary, a crushing responsibility.

In his "Notes for the Biography of George Wythe," written in 1820, Thomas Jefferson summarized Wythe's professional temperament:

> *[He] went early to the bar of the General Court, then occupied by men of great ability, learning, and dignity in their profession. He soon became eminent among them, and, in process of time, the first at the bar, taking into consideration his superior learning, correct elocution, and logical style of reasoning; for in pleading he never indulged himself with an useless or declamatory thought or word; and became as distinguished by correctness and purity of conduct in his profession, as he was by his industry and fidelity to those who employed him.*

During his apprenticeship, Wythe had an oportunity to witness the legal system in action on periodic court days at area county seats. Compared to today's largely decorous courtroom proceedings, trials took place in often unruly settings. Colonial court days provided an opportunity for farmers and their families to come to town to rub elbows with the gentry, gossip, and shop.

Court proceedings, especially murder trials, served as high entertainment. In hot months, the small redbrick courthouses were filled with unwashed, pungent bodies and whiskey flowed freely. Popular lawyers like Patrick Henry took the stage, full of drama and bombast, but their arguments often revealed a serious lack of legal training. They frequently won cases before a jury or judge on pure theatrics. Judges ran the show, but sometimes they were as poorly educated as the attorneys.

At the dawn of the new nation, Wythe and Jefferson had numerous conversations about qualifications for judges. America's court system was ripe for reform and expansion. It was imperative that ethical, educated judges fill the new positions.

In 1776, Jefferson wrote to Wythe:

The judges. . .should always be men of learning and experience in the laws, of exemplary morals, great patience, calmness and attention; their

> *minds should not be distracted with jarring in-*
> *terests; they should not be dependent upon any*
> *man or body of men. To these ends they should*
> *hold estates for life in their offices, or, in other*
> *words, their commissions should be during good*
> *behavior, and their salaries ascertained and es-*
> *tablished by law.* [3]

In Virginia, judges have fixed terms and can be reappointed by the General Assembly, assuming good behavior (impartial, being of sound mind). They do not run for office in public elections. Jefferson may have feared that judges running periodically for their jobs would become beholden to campaign donors, partisan politics, and special money interests, losing their needed objectivity. Today, twenty-one states have chosen to have their judges run for office, including such states as Texas where judges campaign according to party label, presuming certain partisan predispositions in advance.

Envisioning America's future court system, James Madison hoped for "a bench happily filled" with the likes of George Wythe, John Blair, and Edmund Pendleton, leading Virginia jurists of Madison's day. Each was esteemed for his judicial temperament and ethical principles.

At the beginning of America's nationhood, both Wythe and Jefferson feared abuse of power in government. Forward thinkers among the Founding Fathers began to talk more and more about establishing a necessary system of checks and balances within the organizational structure. This could be achieved by having three branches of government, with an independent judiciary.

The excellent administration of justice, in Jefferson's mind, depended to a large extent on the example set for future judges by older judges and teachers. Beverly Tucker, a former Wythe student who later served as a judge and professor of law at William & Mary, noted that talent in the legal field was abundant, "but a learned lawyer was indeed a *rara avis*"—a rare bird.

He observed that in the "loose practice" of law prevailing at the time, "there was but one man in the State who had any claims to the character [of a learned man]. I speak of the venerable Chancellor Wythe, a man who differed from his contemporaries in this, because in his ordinary motives and modes of action he differed altogether from other men. Without ambition, without avarice. . . his active mind found its only enjoyment in profound research." [4]

Wythe biographer Dice Robins Anderson wrote of the professor's character as a model for law students: "Not one dirty coin ever reached the bottom of Wythe's pockets. But of one thing we may be certain that there was never a breath of scandal about the legal career of George Wythe from the time he began to practice in 1746 . . . down to 1806 when he died." [5]

Reflecting these principles, Wythe wrote an oath of office for judges of Virginia's Court of the Admiralty in the late-1770's that reverberates today in Virginia's Canons of Judicial Conduct, an early model for other states. Understanding that corruption could invade the judiciary without firmly established high standards of conduct, he wrote:

"You shall swear that . . . you will do equal right to all manner of people, great and small, high and low, rich and poor, according to equity and good conscience, and the laws and usages of Virginia, without respect to persons . . . And, finally . . . you shall faithfully, justly and truly . . . do equal and impartial justice, without fraud, favor or affection, or partiality." Additionally, judges were forbidden to take "any gift, fee, or reward of gold, silver or any other thing, directly or indirectly." Wythe also provided detailed plans for Virginia's new Court of Appeals.

As a classical scholar, Wythe chose a grim reminder of judicial integrity when he designed a new seal for his High Court of Chancery. According to the Greek historian Herodotus, a Persian judge named Sisamnes was punished for taking a bribe. Making him an example for others, King Cambyses had the judge killed and his skin peeled away, cut into strips, and stretched on the base of the judicial throne. He then appointed the judge's son to succeed him. In that seat of justice, framed by his father's example, the younger man would always be reminded of the hard lesson of honesty. [6]

While Wythe taught numerous future judges at the state and national level, United States Supreme Court Chief Justice John Marshall was the brightest star in Wythe's firmament of judicial achievers. Born in 1755 in modest circumstances, Marshall lacked access to formal education during his youth, as had Wythe. Also, like Wythe, he compensated by devouring books in available libraries.

The best of his formal education occurred when he enrolled in the William & Mary Law School where he absorbed Wythe's philosophy not only about the law but also about government. Some of Marshall's notes from his time in Wythe's classroom showed that he was an attentive law student.

But he was also a mature young man of twenty-five, returning from the battlefield as one of George Washington's trusted officers, and thoughts of love and marriage were also top of mind. He was especially interested in getting on in life with Miss Mary Ambler of Richmond; his notes from Wythe's class are filled with scribbles of variations of her name.

Although he attended classes for fewer than two months, his exposure to Wythe as teacher and high-ranking judge laid the groundwork for Marshall's notable legal career. When not in Wythe's classroom, he read on his own the new Code of Virginia laws that Wythe and Jefferson helped to write, Blackstone's *Commentaries*, and Matthew Bacon's *New Abridgment*. He made extensive notes, organizing information into subject headings, in a "commonplacing" of some of the more difficult material.

Prior to his appointment as Chief Justice, Marshall served as Attorney General of Virginia, Congressman in the United States House of Representatives, and as the nation's fourth Secretary of State. In 1801, President John Adams nominated him as fourth Chief Justice of the Supreme Court.

He held this office for thirty-four years, the longest service of any chief justice in American history. His opinions elevated the Supreme Court to a level of enormous power, promoted nationalism, and laid the foundation for American constitutional law.

As the nation's chief judge, Marshall drew insight from rulings that Virginia's Judge George Wythe had made earlier. Chief among these was the case of *Commonwealth v. Caton* (1782). When he served as an ex-officio member of the Virginia Supreme Court, Judge Wythe first asserted the fundamental concepts of separation of powers within the branches of government and judicial review, the power of courts to rule on laws deemed unconstitutional.

In 1803, Chief Justice John Marshall would follow Wythe's lead in one of Marshall's most important cases, *Marbury v. Madison*. This seminal ruling officially affirmed the model of judicial review and separation of powers in American government. In the future, there would be a stronger balance of power among the legislative, judicial, and executive branches.

Professor Wythe's influence can also be seen in Marshall's sartorial choices for serving on the high bench. Judge Wythe presided in a plain black robe, honoring the purity of justice and perhaps reflecting his forebears' Quaker values of simplicity and humility. On his first day at the Supreme Court in 1801, Marshall arrived similarly dressed, to the amazement of the sitting judges.

Mimicking high court judges in the Old World, they had arrayed themselves in rich red and costly ermine robes, as befitting their august station in life. Beginning with the next session, Marshall's plain black gown became the order of the day, a modest act setting the tone for the Supreme Court's role as final interpreter of the Constitution. Succeeding generations followed the plain style, garnished by Ruth Bader Ginsberg's lace collars in the twenty-first century.

Two of George Wythe's students, Marshall and Bushrod Washington, a nephew of George Washington, served on the Supreme Court at the same time. From 1798 until his death in 1829, Washington was an influential force as an associate judge, championing a strong national government with Marshall. He was only thirty-six when appointed to the court and joined Marshall in ruling on a number of landmark cases. Earlier, he had served as a member of the Virginia House of Delegates from Westmoreland County.

Wythe himself was offered a federal judgeship when the federal court system was first organized during George Washington's presidency. At the time, a judgeship in Virginia—large, wealthy, and influential—was considered more important than a post in the fledgling new national system. Wythe chose to remain at the state level. William & Mary graduates, however, began to fill high federal judgeships as they opened.

Only a few years out of law school, Spencer Roane was appointed judge of the Virginia General Court, then moved to become a consequential judge of the Virginia Supreme Court of Appeals, alongside fellow William & Mary graduate John Coulter. Unlike Wythe's students John Marshall and Bushrod Washington, who championed a strong national government, Roane was the country's leading judge defending states' rights. One of Wythe's most brilliant pupils, he was also the nation's most famous strict-constructionist jurist. Had the choice of chief justice been Jefferson's rather than that of his predecessor, John Adams, it is possible that Roane's imprint would have been on American history, rather than Marshall's.

Among other William & Mary graduates who served as judges were John Louis Taylor, the first chief justice of the Supreme Court of Appeals of North Carolina, and Buckner Thruston and Joseph Clay, both appointed United States Circuit Court judges. Clay also served as a Federal District judge.

When teaching his students the importance of judicial ethics, Professor Wythe would have warned of the possibilities of bribery. In his judicial career, Wythe was known to return expensive gifts sent as bribes. He also declined gifts and excess compensation from clients who wanted to express their gratitude for his legal services.

He made a comfortable living as an attorney and lived well in Williamsburg, but he could easily have doubled his income by cutting a few ethical corners. In early 1807 after Wythe's death, a writer for the *American Gleaner and Virginia Magazine* noted that "strange as it may seem to the lawyers of the present day . . . he never undertook the support of a cause which he knew to be bad, and, if he discovered his client had deceived him, returned him the fee and forsook it." This seldom happened, though, because Wythe was "extremely particular in questioning every person who applied to employ him." He wouldn't work with the client unless the case appeared to be "just and honorable."

Further, when he had doubts, he insisted that his client make an affidavit to the truth of the case, and he examined witnesses for facts to be proved before agreeing to take on the cause. The writer then editorialized: "If the gentlemen of the bar would always follow this rule, how much injustice and oppression would be prevented, how much troublesome and useless litigation would be avoided!" [7]

The Reverend Charles A. Goodrich, an early biographer, summarized Wythe's mindset: "An ardent desire to promote the happiness of his fellow men, by supporting the cause of justice, and maintaining and establishing their rights, appears to have been his ruling passion. As a judge, he was remarkable for his rigid impartiality, and sincere attachment for the principles of equity; for his fast and various learning; and for his strict and unwearied attention to business. Superior to popular prejudices, and every corrupting influence, nothing could induce him to swerve from truth and right. In his decisions, he seemed to be a pure intelligence, untouched by human passions, and settling disputes of men according to the dictates of eternal and immutable justice." [8]

Wythe appeared to be unmoved by popular opinion, even to the point of becoming unpopular for his controversial decisions, especially those affecting the pocketbooks of his contemporaries. One opinion in particular infuriated some of his establishment colleagues.

After the Revolution, numerous Virginians and others owed debts incurred before the war to British merchants and other English creditors. Many argued that their obligation was no longer valid following the Revolution. Some Virginians attempted to pay their outstanding bills to Englishmen by reimbursing the state's loan office with inflated paper money, which, in Wythe's mind, was "a license to rob Peter for enriching Paul."

In *Page v. Pendleton & Lyons* in 1793, Patrick Henry represented the side of those hoping to be free of their lingering debts to British creditors. Henry argued with emotion and eloquence for Virginia debtors, many impoverished by the Revolution and by a disastrous post-war economic depression. An agent representing those to whom money was owed said that Henry displayed "all of his declamatory talents" to "inflame mens minds, prevent their Judgments, and drive them to acts of Outrage."

Henry's orations angered Judge Wythe, who spoke disparagingly of arguments meant to "prove that an American citizen might honestly as well as profitably withhold money which he owned to a british subject." Observing the admiration and adulation that Henry received for championing a reneging on debts, Wythe said that observers might have suspected that one of the cardinal virtues (honesty) "either is not cultivated in America, or is not understood to be the same there as it is in all other civilized countries." [9]

In his ruling, Wythe continued to hammer home his insistence that judges be absolutely impartial: "A judge should not be susceptible to national antipathy, more than of malice towards individuals—whilst executing his office, he should not be more affected by patriotic considerations." Writing fifty years after Wythe's death, Hugh Blair Grigsby said that Wythe did not have "that miserable fear of risking popularity" that "haunts the daily as well as the nightly visions of the modern politician."[10]

"Wythe's reputation for boldness, originality, earning, and integrity was well founded," noted Dice Robins Anderson. "If [John] Marshall was correct in saying that an ignorant, corrupt, and dependent judiciary are the greatest curse that could afflict a people, we should be willing to contend that wise, righteous, and fearless judges, like Wythe, are the most treasured possessions of a free people."[11]

Years before Wythe heard Patrick Henry's arguments in *Page v. Pendleton & Lyons,* Wythe had served on a panel granting law licenses in Virginia and had great reservations about endorsing Henry's application in 1760. While Henry proved to be a brilliant orator, bordering on rabble-rousing, his legal education was scanty. It is believed that Henry became a lawyer through self-study, since there are no records that he had been an apprentice to any other attorney. Thomas Jefferson was especially critical of his lack of education and complained that in matters of law, his judgement was "not worth a copper." [12]

In Wythe's mind, with regard to Henry's stance in *Page v Pendleton & Lyons*, violating a property agreement, a contract, or a commercial obligation was to "violate the most sacred aspect of civilized life."[13] On several important occasions Wythe entered decrees for large sums of money against his native state. "Yet, to the immortal honor of the people of Virginia, be it said, those decisions did not diminish his popularity, but made them admire and respect him still more than ever," stated William Munford at Wythe's funeral.

Munford noted that it was "not uncommon to hear notable contrasts drawn between some unworthy judges who have soiled the judicial ermine and brought their decisions and illegal acts into disrepute and themselves into contempt." By comparison to such judges, Munford emphasized, society should hold Wythe up as an "exemplar" of all that is worthy in the profession. [14]

Chapter Five
Mentorship: "A brain to pick, an ear to listen, and a push in the right direction"

"I had the good fortune to become acquainted very early with some characters of very high standing, and to feel the incessant wish that I could even become what they were."

—Thomas Jefferson [1]

William & Mary and its Law School, among others, offer opportunities for students to learn from experienced mentors. In many cases, the guidance and friendship of a senior advisor can provide life-altering benefits.

Before the establishment of America's first law school in Williamsburg, private mentorship, or apprenticeship, was the prevailing form of legal education. Apprenticeship education continued to be the norm for many years afterward for those who could not attend law school.

Several noteworthy individuals, including Thomas Jefferson and Henry Clay, received the benefit of a William & Mary Law School education outside of the campus classroom. With a love of teaching, George Wythe mentored at least a dozen youth in his home office over a period of years. To many of these young men, he became a beloved father figure and wise advisor

Between 1762 and 1779, he taught seven future leaders, including Thomas Jefferson, in his home in Williamsburg; nearly two hundred more, including John Marshall, in his classroom at the College of William & Mary from 1779 to 1789; and an additional five, including Henry Clay, in his Richmond home from 1790 to 1806.

It is little known that Thomas Jefferson was not necessarily on a leadership track during his formative years and was in need of his own private leadership training program. He arrived in Williamsburg to attend the College of William & Mary in 1760 at the end of his sixteenth year, largely unsupervised. He had lost his much-loved and admired father, Peter, two years earlier and then drifted for a time without a strong adult role model.

On his own, with a teenager's appetite for adventure, he explored all that the busy colonial capital, which he once termed "Devilsburg," had to offer. While he was a good student, he also spent some of his early college days with gamblers, card sharps, and others in the sporting crowd—underachievers with limited horizons. Looking back on that time in 1808, he described a crossroad in his life in a letter to his grandson Thomas Jefferson Randolph.[2]

> *When I consider that at fourteen years of age the whole care and direction of myself was thrown on myself entirely, without a relative or a friend qualified to advise or guide me, and recollect the various sorts of bad company with which I associated from time to time, I am astonished that I did not turn off with some of them, and become as worthless to society as they were. From the circumstances of my position, I was often thrown into the society of horseracers, cardplayers, foxhunters, scientific and professional men, and of dignified men; and many a time have I asked myself, in the enthusiastic death of a fox, the victory of a favorite horse, the issue of a question eloquently argued at the bar, or in the great council of the nation, 'Well, which of these kinds of reputation should I prefer—that of a horse jockey, a*

*foxhunter, an orator, or the honest advocate of my
country's rights?'*

Like Jefferson, his grandson was heading off on
his own at an impressionable age. Jefferson warned
him: "Your dangers are great, and still your safety
must rest on yourself. A determination never to do
what is wrong, prudence, and good humor, will go
far towards securing you the estimation of the
world." His heartfelt advice included examples
from his own youth. After recalling that gambling
and sporting men might have led him down the
wrong path, he wrote:

*I had the good fortune to become acquainted very
early with some characters of very high standing,
and to feel the incessant wish that I could even
become what they were. Under temptations and
difficulties, I could ask myself what would Dr.
Small, Mr. Wythe, Peyton Randolph [a distinguished older relative] do in this situation? What
course in it will ensure me their approbation? I
am certain that this mode of deciding on my conduct tended more to its correctness than any rea-
soning powers I possessed. Knowing the even and
dignified line they pursued, I could never doubt*

for a moment which of two courses would be in
character for them. . . . with the jaundiced eye of
youth, I should often have erred."

Reviewing his mid-teens, Jefferson seemed to have understood his vulnerability at the time—lacking mature guidance and associating with adults of dubious character. At some point during his seven-year educational experience in Williamsburg, he made a critical choice regarding how he would spend his time. He left behind more trivial pursuits, threw himself into his studies, learned to debate in courtroom and legislative forums, and began to connect with "scientific, professional, and dignified men."

Chief among these were George Wythe, under whom he studied for five years as Wythe's legal apprentice; William Small, Jefferson's undergraduate professor for two years, an important mentor who nurtured his love of the sciences and Enlightenment philosophy; and Colonial English Governor Francis Fauquier, at whose elegant dinner table young Jefferson joined in the company of sophisticated, educated, and principled adults.

George Wythe, in particular, would help to radicalize the youth, teaching him to become, in

Jefferson's words, an "honest advocate of my country's rights." Of Wythe, Jefferson recalled fondly: "He was my ancient master, my earliest and best friend." Wythe became the man to whom Jefferson was most indebted for "first impressions which have had the most salutary influence on the course of my life."[3]

In a biographical sketch of Wythe, Jefferson recalled: "He directed my studies in the law, led me into business, and continued, until death, my most affectionate friend. Observing Wythe's character, Jefferson continued: "The exalted virtue of the man will be a polar star to guide you in all matters which may touch that element of his character. As far as I know, he never had an enemy." [4]

Jefferson probably met Wythe sometime in his seventeenth year, introduced by Professor Small, who had taken the youth under his wing. Jefferson was bright and played a mean fiddle, making him a suitable guest at the Governor's Palace which he frequented with Small and Wythe as guests of English Governor William Fauquier.

As a member of this "quartet," as he called it, Jefferson played music, polished his manners, listened to the news of the day, and discussed literature, philosophy, and ethics with the older men.

The men also had an intense interest in new scientific developments. They enjoyed sharing with Jefferson their interests in astronomy, the weather, mathematics, paleontology, scientific agriculture, medicine, education, antiquities, physics, history, religion, government, art, architecture, natural law, and numerous other subjects.

These senior mentors introduced the young man from rural Albemarle County to a wider world. Jefferson later recalled evenings at the palace as filled with good music and some of the best conversations he ever enjoyed. Experiencing the elegant dinners in witty, intellectual company would serve him well later when he played host to his own gatherings as minister to France and as president of the United States.

After completing his undergraduate studies at William & Mary, Jefferson asked Wythe to mentor him in the law as his apprentice. Wythe ran a tight ship in his leadership training curriculum. The academic schedule with Jefferson often ran from before dawn until well after dark. A fellow Virginian, the late United States Supreme Court Justice Lewis F. Powell, Jr., noted: "In sum, the tutelage under Wythe was the equivalent for Jefferson of the most exacting of university educations—indeed, far more demanding than what is called a university education today." [5]

As Wythe's apprentice, Jefferson had the job of assisting the attorney with details of his expansive law practice. His good handwriting supported Wythe's volumes of documentation. His quick mind and research capabilities helped the senior lawyer prepare complicated cases. He could be trusted to do a good job.

Once they completed their preparations, they traveled together to court. There Jefferson watched attorneys match wits and judges mete out rulings. Wythe would have explained every legal step to his student. As Jefferson grew in experience and knowledge, his supervisor turned more and more responsibility over to him. Eventually, Jefferson handled cases on his own.

In addition to office work, Wythe assigned his pupil lengthy reading assignments, covering all aspects of the law, ancient and modern, English and Colonial. Not confining his mentorship to the study of law, Wythe expected Jefferson to be thoroughly exposed to every important subject that an educated man should know, with assignments in philosophy, government, history, literature, religion, politics, rhetoric, physics, languages, mathematics, agriculture, architecture, chemistry, music, astronomy, botany, anatomy, zoology, and other wide-ranging subjects not then found at his alma mater.

Wythe and other intellectuals in Williamsburg were members of the Virginia Society for the Promotion of Useful Knowledge. They looked forward to each new shipment of books and newspapers from across the Atlantic so they could review significant new experiments and scientific theories. On their own shores, they kept up with the scientific endeavors of Benjamin Franklin, a corresponding member of their group. Williamsburg's amateur scientists studied the skies with their telescopes, recorded seasonal changes, and kept detailed records of the growth of crops and other living things.

Jefferson observed the older men in their ongoing studies and later meticulously kept his own daily records at Monticello. On a clear night, Wythe and his friends would take their telescopes into the quiet of their gardens. In the inky black skies of the pre-electric, pre-industrial age, they could see glorious firmaments, vast tapestries of brilliant lights scattered across a great dark dome. Like Wythe, Jefferson would fill his own home with telescopes and numerous other scientific devices, sharing a boundless curiosity about the workings of the natural world.

Wythe's influence can be traced to Jefferson's greatest lifetime achievements, those he wished to be engraved on his tombstone: author of the Declaration of Independence, author of the Virginia Statute for Religious Freedom, and father of the University of Virginia, where Jefferson tried to replicate a close student-teacher relationship and comprehensive curriculum.

During Jefferson's first year of practice in 1767, Wythe introduced him to Virginia's highest court, the General Court. He also asked the new lawyer to assist him in several major cases, furthering Jefferson's career. Jefferson frequently asked Wythe for an opinion on legislative or legal matters. Only two years later, Wythe as clerk of Virginia's House of Burgesses, had the pleasure of swearing in Jefferson as the recently elected representative for the County of Albemarle, beginning Jefferson's long political career.

William Wirt, who knew both men, summarized the influence of Wythe's legal training on the mind of Thomas Jefferson:

The study of the law he pursued under George Wythe; a man of Roman Stamp, in Rome's best age. Here he acquired that unrivaled neatness, system and method in business, which through all his life, and in every office that he filled, gave him, in effect, the hundred hands of Briareus [a character from Greek mythology with fifty heads and a hundred arms, the son of Heaven and Earth, who got things done, a reference to Jefferson's legendary multi-tasking skills]; here too, following the giant steps of his master, he traveled the whole round of civil and common law. From the same example [Wythe], he caught that untiring spirit of investigation which never left a subject till he had searched it to the bottom. In short, Mr. Wythe placed on his head the crown of legal preparation: and well did it become him.[6]

While more than a hundred miles of difficult roads separated Jefferson's home in Albemarle County from Wythe's in Williamsburg, they maintained a close friendship until Wythe's death. In letters, they talked about new books to read and new plants to try in their gardens. They shared seed catalogues, the works of ancient Greek and Roman writers, and even esoteric religious writings such as the *Olympiads*, rare diaries from the early Christian period. At Monticello, the Jefferson family dined on a large, beautiful mahogany Rococo table that their descendants called the "Wythe table," said to have been a wedding gift from Jefferson's old friend.

Over the years, Jefferson and Wythe collaborated on numerous projects. They shared a love of historic legal scholarship. In the early 1790s, Judge Wythe sought Jefferson's advice about artwork and words for a new seal that Wythe had proudly designed for his High Court of Chancery. Wythe trusted Jefferson's judgment about the seal's classical theme and about how best to have it professionally rendered.

During his service as Speaker of the Virginia House of Delegates, Wythe presided by carefully studying and following established rules of parliamentary procedure—something few of his peers had bothered to master. By 1800, Jefferson found himself in immediate need of Wythe's expertise. As Vice President of the United States, Jefferson served as presiding officer of the United States Senate. At the time, Congress had no set rules for order and decorum when the group met to discuss the nation's business.

Jefferson's challenge: how to tame a legislative circus of strong egos and colliding opinions. He considered Wythe the only remaining source of parliamentary procedure to call upon and sent him a list of questions about various proposed procedures. Jefferson incorporated Wythe's advice and that of others such as Edmund Pendleton in a *Manual on Parliamentary Practice for the Use of the Senate*, printed in 1801. The Senate used his manual for a number of decades.

As a last tribute to Wythe, Jefferson suggested that his daughter, Martha, name her baby son George Wythe Randolph. In his proposal for a prototype community college system for Virginia, Jefferson wanted the first to bear the name of George Wythe. Jefferson's system was never funded in his lifetime, but more than a century later, Wytheville Community College was founded in Wytheville, Virginia, county seat of Wythe County, all named in honor of Jefferson's teacher.

In addition to mentoring Jefferson in Wythe's home on Palace Green, Wythe coached another legal apprentice, St. George Tucker, who succeeded him as William & Mary's second professor of law and went on to become a justice of the Virginia Supreme Court and judge of the U.S. District

Court for the Eastern District of Virginia.

Another legal apprentice, the Reverend James Madison, second cousin of the president by that name, was one of the few Wythe students not to follow a career in the law. An agent of change, he served two major institutions during times of enormous transition, as president of the College of William & Mary from 1777 to 1812 and as the first Episcopal bishop of the Diocese of Virginia, following disestablishment of the state's official religion, the Anglican Church, after the Revolution.

In addition to legal apprentices, Wythe mentored a number of other young men who studied in his house from time to time. Three of them, Henry Clay, Littleton Waller Tazewell, and William Munford, wrote extensively of their time with their teacher.

Clay was the last of Wythe's national super stars and belonged to the generation following the Founding Fathers. He was born in 1777 during the Revolution and enjoyed the liberties and opportunities that were unfolding in the new nation. Like George Wythe, he had lost his father at an early age. Clay was only three when his father, John, died at thirty-eight, leaving behind an unborn baby and six other young children. Like Thomas Jefferson,

Clay met George Wythe during his adolescence when he was most in need of a mentor.

By the time their paths crossed, Wythe had moved to the new state capital in Richmond in 1791 to become judge of Virginia's High Court of Chancery. Young Clay had left his family farm in nearby Hanover County to begin life in the city, remaining in Virginia after his stepfather and mother announced plans to move to Kentucky to try their luck on the frontier.

Clay took a job as an assistant clerk in Virginia's High Court of Chancery. After being noted for his careful penmanship, he became Wythe's stenographer and private secretary, assisting with high volumes of paperwork. At the time, Judge Wythe was in his late sixties and had begun to suffer from arthritis in his right hand.

Clay worked carefully and diligently, and Wythe was pleased with his thoroughness, willing attitude, and sunny personality. During four years of employment, Clay became a companion for the childless widower as well as his capable secretary. With no home of his own, Clay made Wythe's house his home and availed himself of his employer's magnificent library. During this time, Wythe led Clay into the wider world of literature, philosophy, politics, culture, and social comportment. Together, they studied nobility of character, ethics, and statesmanship. Like Wythe at his age, Clay worked hard to improve himself through constant study.

At the end of four years, the former farm boy had acquired enough polish and ambition to aspire to become a lawyer. Wythe asked a friend, Virginia Attorney General Robert Brooke, to take Clay into his office as a legal apprentice. Brooke had recently completed a term as Virginia governor and was eminently well-connected.

The Hanover youth who had come to Richmond with limited prospects only a few years earlier became at age twenty Henry Clay, Esquire, with a respected law license and excellent recommendations. He left Richmond in 1797 for what was then America's frontier in Kentucky.

Clay immediately connected with three other Wythe protégés in Kentucky, John Breckinridge, James Brown, and George Nicholas. All four would have outstanding legal and political careers, and all four would continue Wythe's legacy by teaching new generations of attorneys as university law professors in Kentucky. Clay served as a law professor and member of the board of trustees of Transylvania University, the first college west of the Al-

legheny Mountains. He married and named his
first son Theodore Wythe Clay.

Mentored in Wythe's anti-slavery beliefs, Clay
freed all of the slaves that he held at the time of
his death. Known as the "Great Compromiser" for
his diplomatic skills, he was elected three times
Speaker of the United States House of Representatives before beginning a legendary career in the
United States Senate. He also served as Secretary
of State under President John Quincy Adams.

Clay paid a high price for his efforts to hold the
Union together and to resolve slavery issues. Normally, he would have been at the top of his party's
ticket for president of the United States. After a
particularly acrimonious debate in 1838 when he
took a principled but unpopular stand, he is fa-
mously quoted as saying, "I'd rather be right than
be president." 7

Clay was among seven former Wythe acolytes
to become governor of a state. Another, Littleton
Waller Tazewell, became a U.S. senator and U.S.
representative as well as Governor of Virginia. A
Williamsburg boy, he was among Wythe's youngest
pupils, beginning his schooling in Wythe's house at
the age of twelve. Wythe wanted to give him the
best education possible, as he was the grandson of

Benjamin Waller, Wythe's benefactor when he moved to Williamsburg as a young lawyer.

In his memoirs as an old man, Tazewell noted that Wythe's "mode of instruction was singular, and as everything connected with the life and opinions of this great and good man, must be interesting," describing his time with the teacher. "Interesting" was the salient word. Wythe tried to make science interesting for Tazewell and the study of law interesting for his older law students.[8]

In Williamsburg and later when they moved together to Richmond, Wythe would mentor another young man, William Munford, from less fortunate circumstances than Tazewell's. Born in Mecklenburg County, Virginia, at the cusp of the Revolution in 1775, Munford lost his father, a war veteran, when he was seven. His impoverished mother taught Munford at home until the boy needed further education and sought George Wythe's tutoring services, but lacked funds for tuition. Wythe, without a child of his own, took the youth into his home at his own expense, providing a comprehensive education and a father-like mentorship.

As an adult, Munford became an influential member and Clerk of the Virginia House of Delegates, Virginia state senator, member of the Virginia Council of State, reporter for the Virginia Supreme Court of Appeals, and noted revisor of Virginia laws.

Next to Jefferson, Munford probably spent the most time in Wythe's presence. Wythe taught Munford in his home and gave Munford a place to live there in the youth's time of need. Munford recalled, "Chancellor Wythe is the best friend I ever had, and one of the most remarkable men I ever knew, and he certainly has been as kind to me as a father." [9]

Wythe's mentorship transcended race and class. Munford wrote to a friend that Wythe was teaching another student at the same time: "Would you believe it, he has begun to teach Jimmy, his servant to write? Nevertheless, it is true, and is only one more example of that benignity, granted by heaven to the minds of a few." After preparing Jimmy with an education, Wythe released him from slavery in 1797. In his older years, Wythe would devote enormous energy and love to teaching Michael Brown, a mixed-race boy and a freed slave, in his household in Richmond.

Writing fifty years after Wythe's death, biographer Charles Goodrich appeared puzzled about why such a successful man would take time from his busy career for the "generally unpleasant task of the education of youth." Of Wythe's private tutoring, he wrote:

Yet, even to this, he was prompted by his genuine patriotism and philanthropy, which induced him for many years to take great delight in educating such young persons as showed an inclination for improvement. Harassed as he was with business, and enveloped with papers belonging to intricate suits in chancery, he yet found time to keep a private school for the instruction of a few scholars, always with very little compensation, and often demanding none. Several living ornaments of their country received their greatest lights from his sublime example and instruction. Such was the upright and venerable Wythe.[10]

In describing Wythe as his "faithful and beloved Mentor in youth, and my most affectionate friend throughout life," Jefferson capitalized the word "Mentor."[11] Memorialized in Homer's Odyssey, Mentor was a friend of the wandering Odysseus, who entrusted Mentor with the role of educating his son Telemachus.

Good mentorship, like good parenting, is known to be passed down to the next generation. Wythe, seventeen years older, mentored Jefferson in the ideals of leadership, statesmanship, and service to country. Jefferson in turn mentored these principles for the younger Founding Fathers, James Monroe, fifteen years his junior, and James Madison, eight years younger than Jefferson.

Nineteenth-century statesman and jurist John C. Crosby defined mentorship as "a brain to pick, an ear to listen, and a push in the right direction," and Wythe and Jefferson proved adept in each of these regards.

Chapter Six
The Question of
Slavery and the Murder of
George Wythe

"Freedom is the birthright of
every human being."

—George Wythe, 1806 court ruling

Students entering William & Mary's Law
School between 1779 and 1789 were soon given a
solid dose of anti-slavery sentiment from their professor. Wythe was determined to upend the pro-
slavery belief system, when given the opportunity.
He was clearly out of step with the establishment,
cut from a different cloth.

During the last year of his life in 1806, as judge
of Virginia's High Court of Chancery, he broke
legal precedent by declaring slavery illegal, based
on Virginia's Declaration of Rights. The ruling was
overturned by a higher court, but it was his principled stab at the entrenched institution. Wythe's in-
clusion of several former slaves in his will played
into the scenario of his murder that same year by a

deranged nephew looking for an early inheritance.

Most of Wythe's students and colleagues came from families schooled in the Anglican faith, the Church of England. Since the first days of Virginia settlement, this was the official religion, and it held conservative views regarding the rights of slave owners. Wythe, on the other hand, came from a family of independent Quaker thinkers, with a strong anti-slavery heritage.

His great-grandfather, George Keith, had traveled to America as a Quaker evangelist. He was a well-educated Scotsman, full of zeal. When visiting Quakers in Pennsylvania in the 1690's, he excoriated some of the faithful for owning slaves. In 1693, he wrote what is likely the country's first anti-slavery treatise. It is probable that Wythe had studied it and given a copy to his friend Benjamin Franklin, who published the pamphlet on his Philadelphia press.

While most of the South steadfastly defended the institution, Jefferson was quick to point out that future leaders taught by George Wythe might be open to reform. In a letter to British abolitionist Dr. Richard Price in 1785, Jefferson described American sentiments regarding slavery. As author of the Declaration of Independence, he was often on the defensive about questions of slave ownership. Price had written a paper condemning slavery's abominations. His treatise was circulating throughout the country, and he asked Jefferson about its reception.

Jefferson told Price that few readers in the South would agree with his ideas, but that a new generation, steeped in revolutionary liberty, might be more willing to address the problem. He then remarked on Professor Wythe's influence on his students:

> *The College of William and Mary in Williamsburg, since the remodeling of its plan, is the place where are collected together all the young men of Virginia under preparation for public life. They are there under the direction (most of them) of a Mr. Wythe, one of the most virtuous of characters, and whose sentiments on the subject of slavery are unequivocal. I am satisfied if you could resolve to address an exhortation to those young men, with all that eloquence of which you are master, that its influence on the future decision of this important question would be great, perhaps decisive.*[1]

In a letter to Jean Nicolas Demeunier in June of 1786, Jefferson wrote of changes in attitude about slavery among some future Virginia leaders being trained by Professor Wythe for public life:

The disposition to emancipate them [in five southern states] is strongest in Virginia. Those who desire it, form as yet the minority of the whole state, but it bears a respectable proportion to the whole in numbers and weight of character, and it is continually recruiting by the addition of nearly the whole of the young men as fast as they come into public life.[2]

Although many of his students like Jefferson never freed their slaves, the professor managed to make his charges feel guilty about participating in the institution. Some like Jefferson proposed emancipation laws and others formed organizations to free, educate, and repatriate slaves. Few left Wythe's classroom unaffected by his firm belief that everyone is entitled to freedom.

An ardent opponent of slavery in young adulthood, it is unlikely that Jefferson harbored antislavery views before coming under Wythe's guidance in his late teens. Later, as a new member of the Virginia legislature, Jefferson supported a law to end slavery gradually, a law that he and

Wythe had discussed. Jefferson was shocked, astounded, by the vicious rejection of the idea by establishment legislators.

As president, he supported a law in 1807 to end the importation of slaves from abroad. By then, however, the institution had become entrenched, and the domestic breeding of slaves for sale thrived as a lucrative business. It is thought in some quarters that Jefferson would have freed his slaves if he could have afforded to do so. He died in serious debt.

With the realization that emancipation laws faced failure in southern legislatures, some former Wythe students developed an alternate plan. Several leaders, including John Marshall, Henry Clay, James Monroe, and Thomas Jefferson, supported a repatriation program to free slaves, educate them, and send them to their own homeland. While some former slaves left American shores under this arrangement, the plan was expensive and never involved large numbers.

George Wythe had also grappled with the disturbing presence of slavery in his own life. He was born on a plantation worked by slaves. He owned them later as part of his legal inheritance. He married into a slave-holding family. Immediately after his wife died, Wythe freed those household servants who were legally his to release. He also divested himself of his farm with its reliance on slave labor.

He paid devoted former slave, Lydia Broadnax, wages for her continued cooking and cleaning services, purchased a house for her that would provide rental income, and remembered her in his will, along with other former slaves. In his own way, Wythe was trying to compensate for a past that included participation in the institution he despised.

It is unknown how many of Wythe's students eventually emancipated their slaves, stirred by his admonitions. Some, like Henry Clay, freed their remaining slaves in their wills. John Minor, not long after studying under the professor, introduced two bills in the Virginia General Assembly that would have led to the gradual emancipation of slaves. No action was taken. Later, Minor freed all of his slaves and sent them at his own expense to Liberia.

One student, Richard Randolph, took immediate action after leaving Wythe's tutelage in Williamsburg. A member of one of Virginia's most prominent families, Randolph was a conservative parent's nightmare. He had likely left home as an apolitical youth, only to return from college as a full-blown radical, threatening to give away much of the family's valuable property.

Filled with idealistic zeal, Randolph quickly wanted to free the slaves that he had inherited from his father. He found, however, that they were encumbered in the family's serious debt as "property." Perhaps sensing that his slaves would outlive him, Randolph wrote a detailed will freeing them, even though he was only in his twenties. The will read like an anti-slavery treatise, filled with ideals of the Enlightenment, the Declaration of Independence, Virginia's Declaration of Rights, and Wythe's humanitarian beliefs.

Randolph not only granted his slaves their freedom but also generously provided family land for each head of household to farm. Only a few months after the will was finalized, he died at the age of twenty-six. He named as his executors two brothers, his stepfather, and George Wythe, whom he described as "the most virtuous and incorruptible of mankind" and "the brightest ornament of human nature." Eventually, the slaves were given their freedom and farmed the land they were given in Prince Edward County, Virginia, for generations.[3]

Another Wythe student, William Short, had the benefit of extensive foreign travel to broaden his perspectives about race and bondage. An abolitionist, he served as United States Minister to

France, Spain, and the Netherlands. He believed in the natural equality of the races and hoped that future research into African societies and great civilizations would undermine racial prejudice in America. He supported racial intermarriage and became a member of the American Colonization Society, to emancipate, educate, and repatriate slaves to a homeland.

As a teacher, Wythe had been free to advocate abolition to his students. Later, however, as a full-time judge of Virginia's High Court of Chancery, he felt bound by legal precedent. Slavery was established law, time-tested and unquestioned. The law regarded slaves as property—to be purchased and sold in the same manner that a farmer would purchase and sell his horses and cattle.

By 1806 in his eightieth year, Judge Wythe appeared to have become exhausted by having to adjudicate Virginia's laws governing slavery. It is estimated that half of the property cases he heard in his Chancery courtroom involved the disposition of slaves. Like domestic animals, slaves were of economic value in the marketplace. When a man borrowed money or gambled, he could use his servants as collateral. When a slave master died, his servants were part of the legal inheritance of his children, to

109

be divided among them or sold at auction to cover debts. Most of Virginia's planters were debt-ridden; estate slave sales were commonplace.

In rulings before 1806, Judge Wythe had been careful to abide by the law, while giving as much leniency as possible to individuals contesting their freedom. That year, he found an opportunity to test a new ruling: that all individuals are inherently free, based on Virginia's Declaration of Rights.

An opportunity appeared in the case of *Hudgins v. Wright*. At its core, the case was about blood and money—about the genetic content of a slave's blood and about the ability of her owner to benefit economically from her free labor for the rest of her life. Slave woman Jackey Wright sued her owner, Houlder Hudgins, for freedom for herself and her two children. As he owned her, he also owned her offspring and could sell them at will, or work them until their deaths. The future of the Wright family hung in the balance, depending on Wythe's ruling.

Hudgins claimed that Wright was born of a slave mother of African blood and therefore belonged naturally to an enslaved race of people. Wright presented three generations of her family in court. Their physical features appeared to qualify them as part of a free race of people, Native Americans.

Judge Wythe freed her and her two children on two counts. In the first, he concurred that they could be emancipated on the presumed basis of race, of belonging to a free class of people. In the second opinion, he asserted that all individuals were "presumptively free in Virginia," in accordance with the state's Declaration of Rights, published in 1776 and mirroring the ideals of the national Declaration of Independence written around the same time, declaring that all are born free and equally independent.

Wythe wrote that individuals "should be considered free until proven otherwise" and that "freedom is the birthright of every human being." He was the first and only southern judge to rule slavery illegal, based on essential human rights.

A higher court overruled Wythe's second opinion, asserting that Virginia's Declaration of Rights did not include the enslaved and that the right to own slaves as property was established law. Jackey Wright and her two children, however, achieved their freedom on the basis of their presumed Native American lineage.[4]

It is likely that George Wythe's egalitarian views about people of color contributed to his bizarre death in 1806. For all of his mentorship successes, Wythe's influence was not strong enough to advance the future of one misguided youth. His great-nephew and namesake, George Wythe Sweeney, had been sent to live with Wythe in Richmond during Wythe's late-seventies.

His mother had hoped that some of Wythe's guidance would benefit the wayward boy. Had Sweeney arrived at a younger age, that transformation may have been possible. With no surviving children of his own, Wythe was prepared to offer the youth a world of opportunity and education.

The move, however, came too late. Sweeney was already showing signs of addiction to alcohol and gambling, and Richmond offered ample opportunities for dissolute pursuits. As his gambling debts increased, Sweeney began stealing from Wythe and forging checks on his account. The theft of his prized books and scientific instruments was of far greater distress to Wythe than any monetary loss, and Wythe threatened to reduce the inheritance that he had planned for the boy in his will.

Wythe's housekeeper, Lydia Broadnax, reported seeing Sweeney rummage through Wythe's desk to find the will. He discovered that several people of color, individuals close to Wythe, were named in the will—Lydia, a boy named Michael

Brown whom Wythe was tutoring, and a youth named Benjamin.

Thomas Jefferson was named to receive Wythe's favorite gold-tipped cane, a precious early draft of the Declaration of Independence, and Wythe's splendid library. The people of color named in Wythe's will to receive property or bank stock were slaves he had freed. By honoring them in his will, as if they were somehow equal to his white blood-relative Sweeney, Wythe may have crossed a line in the mind of Sweeney, who likely was a supporter of slavery, as were most of his contemporaries.

Sweeney learned by reading the will that if he outlived them, he would inherit their share. One day in late May of 1806, murder was on his mind when he poured arsenic in the household's morning coffee. Broadnax observed him adding a yellow substance to the liquid, but had no reason to be alarmed at the time.

Michael Brown died within five days, and Lydia was injured, but lived to tell the story. Whether intended or not, the coffee made its way upstairs with George Wythe's breakfast. He died two weeks later, after enduring enormous pain. At one point, he rose from his deathbed to cry, "I am murdered."

Before his death, however, he was able to call his attorney, Edmund Randolph, and had Sweeney eliminated from the will.

Sweeney was never convicted of the murders because all of the eyewitnesses to his bizarre behavior that day were people of color, and no one with African blood could testify against a white individual in court. Richmond physicians, unaccustomed to performing autopsies, misdiagnosed the cause of Wythe's death. Additionally, many felt that the well-respected Wythe family shouldn't be subjected to the additional shame of a protracted legal ordeal. Everyone surmised, however, who had done the deed.[5]

George Wythe has the dubious distinction of being the only signer of the Declaration of Independence to be murdered. It was fitting that he was laid in state in Richmond in the imposing Greek Revival capitol building designed by his surrogate son, Jefferson. Thousands, wearing black armbands, filed by the casket to pay their respects.

His funeral was the largest in Virginia up to that time. Shops closed and dignitaries lined the streets as his horse-drawn cortege made its way up the steep hill to burial in the churchyard of St. John's Church where thirty-one years before he had joined Patrick Henry and other Virginia leaders in calling for a militia to begin the fight for independence.

More than a century later, William & Mary's Law School Dean Oscar Shewmake observed that Wythe's "happy and far-reaching influence" on the affairs of his country was incalculable, although his name was mostly unremembered, his biography unwritten at that time. By the twentieth century, Wythe's body lay in an unmarked grave, while everywhere monuments honored men "whose merits in comparison with his shrink into nothingness."

Wythe's death, he said, gave to the people of Virginia a sense of the "loss of something which could never be replaced." Like George Washington, Wythe left no children from his marriage, "regarding the new republic as his posterity." [6]

Chapter Seven
The William & Mary Law School Leadership Cohort

"Nothing would advance me faster in the world
than the reputation of having been educated by
Mr. Wythe, for such a man as he casts a light
upon all around him." [1]

—William Munford, Student

Graduates of the William & Mary Law School
and others tutored by George Wythe filled America's public offices in the first decades of the country's nationhood. His legacy, as noted previously,
includes direct mentorship of a United States president and indirect mentorship of two other presidents, a vice president, two Supreme Court justices,
including a chief justice, five secretaries of state,
Speaker of the U.S. House of Representatives, two
U.S. attorneys general, several foreign ambassadors,
seven state or territorial governors, three Virginia
Supreme Court justices, and numerous senators,
congressmen, state legislators and judges.

At least six counties are named in his students'
honor: Clay, Hardy, Jefferson, Marshall, and Roane
are located in West Virginia. Two counties bear the
name of former pupil William Branch Giles, one in
Virginia and one in Tennessee. Wythe's name was
given to a new Virginia county in 1789, along with numerous schools, avenues, and streets in several states.

"Wythe taught more American leaders than any
other mortal has since or ever will. No one was his
equal as a force in American law," observed Taylor
Reveley, President Emeritus of the College of
William & Mary and one of Wythe's successors as
Dean of its Law School.[2]

Highlights of the careers of some of his students include: [3]

Thomas Jefferson—President, Vice
President, Secretary of State, Minister to
France, Delegate to the Continental Congress, Governor of Virginia (tutored privately by Wythe).

John Marshall—Chief Justice of the
Supreme Court of the United States, Secretary of State, United States House of Representatives.

Henry Clay—Speaker of the United

States House of Representatives, Secretary of State, United States Senator (tutored privately by Wythe).

James Monroe—It was said by some that Wythe taught Monroe, but records are incomplete. Wythe's influence was distilled, however, through Jefferson's mentorship of Monroe. Monroe's offices include President, Secretary of State, Secretary of War, Governor of Virginia, Minister to the United Kingdom, Minister to France, United States Senator, and Delegate to the Virginia Congress of the Confederation.

Bushrod Washington—Associate Justice of the Supreme Court of the United States, Virginia House of Delegates

John Breckinridge—United States Attorney General, United States Senator, Speaker of the Kentucky House of Representatives, Attorney General of Kentucky

James Breckinridge—Virginia House of Delegates, United States House of Representatives, delegate to the Virginia Constitutional Ratifying Convention, member of the Board of Visitors of the University of Virginia.

St. George Tucker—United States District Court Judge, Virginia Supreme Court Judge, Rector and Law School Dean of the College of William & Mary (tutored privately by Wythe).

William Short—United States Ambassador to France, United States Ambassador to Spain, United States Ambassador to the Netherlands.

John Brown—President pro tempore of the United States Senate, member of the United States House of Representatives, delegate to the Congress of the Confederation, member of the Virginia Senate.

Wilson Cary Nicholas—United States Senator, Governor of Virginia, United States House of Representatives, Virginia House of Delegates.

George Nicholas—Attorney General of Kentucky, Virginia House of Delegates, first professor of law at Transylvania University.

Bishop James Madison—President of the College of William & Mary and Bishop of the Diocese of Virginia of the Episcopal Church (tutored privately by Wythe).

Littleton Waller Tazewell—President
pro tempore of the United States Senate,
Governor of Virginia, United States House
of Representatives, Virginia House of Delegates (tutored privately by Wythe).

William Branch Giles—United States
Senator, Governor of Virginia, United
States House of Representatives, Virginia
House of Delegates.

John Roane—Virginia House of Delegates, United States House of Representatives, Virginia Constitutional Convention
of 1829-1830.

Spencer Roane—Judge of the Virginia
Supreme Court of Appeals, Virginia House
of Delegates, Virginia Council of State.

Samuel Hardy—Delegate to the Continental Congress, Virginia House of Delegates,
Lieutenant Governor of Virginia, subject of a
poetic tribute by Alexander Hamilton.

Archibald Stuart, Judge of the Virginia
General Court, member of the Virginia
House of Delegates and the Virginia Senate,
and Presidential Elector.

George Izard—Governor of the Arkansas Territory, Major General in the War of 1812.

John Coalter—Judge of the Virginia Supreme Court of Appeals.

James Innes—President of the Board of War, American Revolution; Attorney General of Virginia; Virginia House of Delegates.

Harry Innes—Judge of the United States District Court, Kentucky, and Attorney General for the District of Kentucky, advocate of statehood for Kentucky.

William Munford—Member and Clerk of the Virginia House of Delegates, Virginia State Senator, Virginia Council of State (Tutored by Wythe at home).

John Wayles Epps—United States Senator, United States House of Representatives, Virginia House of Delegates.

Buckner Thruston—United States Senator, United States Circuit Court Judge, member of the Virginia Assembly.

John Louis Taylor—first Chief Justice, Supreme Court of North Carolina, representative in the North Carolina House of Commons.

Frances Preston—Member of the United States House of Representatives, the Virginia Senate and House of Delegates, Brigadier General of the Virginia militia.

Joseph Clay, Jr.—Federal district Judge, Federal Fifth Circuit Court Judge.

Edmund Randolph—Secretary of State, United States Attorney General, Governor of Virginia, Attorney General of Virginia (thought to have been tutored privately, but in any case, strongly influenced by Wythe).

IMAGES

George Wythe, America's first law professor, taught ethics and statesmanship in addition to the law. Portrait by David Silvette (1979) College of William & Mary Law School.

A bronze statue of George Wythe in front of the William & Mary Law School, also known as the Marshall-Wythe School of Law. Created by Gordon S. Kray, class of 1973, the statue along with its companion of John Marshall, was dedicated on October 7, 2000. (Courtesy of Wolf Law Library, William & Mary)

Wythe held his regular law school classes in the Wren building on the grounds of the College of William & Mary. After the Battle of Yorktown, the building was damaged during use as a hospital for French soldiers.

Virginia's Colonial Capitol, where professor Wythe trained his William & Mary Law School students in moot courts and mock legislatures.

Local residents filled the seats of the Colonial Capitol on Saturdays as William & Mary Law School students practiced their debating skills for future careers as lawyers and legislators.

Thomas Jefferson was admitted to the Virginia Bar after serving as George Wythe's legal apprentice during a private, five-year tutelage under the senior attorney statesman. (Portrait from The Granger Collection, New York)

John Marshall, the nation's fourth Chief Justice of the Supreme Court, was among the first students to enroll in classes at William & Mary's new Law School.

"George Wythe Reads the Report of Rules," May 28, 1787, U.S. Constitution Bicentennial postal envelope. William & Mary Law School students were the first in America to be trained in constitutional law.

Patrick Henry rallied his followers against ratifying the United States Constitution during Virginia's Ratifying Convention in 1788. William & Mary graduates and Law School graduates provided the margin for approval, with the promise of the addition of a Bill of Rights.

ABOUT THE AUTHOR

From a family of history lovers, Suzanne Munson grew up hearing about the trials of ancestors in seventeenth-century Jamestown and pioneers on Virginia's western frontier. She has a special interest in the American Revolution and the role of America's Founding Fathers in establishing the nation's democratic republic.

While writing her first work of history, *Jefferson's Godfather: The Man Behind the Man*, a biography of George Wythe, she began to uncover insights about Wythe's contributions to the nation that have been lost to time. One of these is that Wythe, America's first professor of law, also created the country's first training program for future statesmen, young leaders schooled in government and ethics at the College of William & Mary.

Another insight gained from research is the conclusion that Wythe's influence was directly behind the three lifetime accomplishments that Jefferson wanted engraved on his tombstone: author of the Declaration of Independence, author of the Virginia Statute for Religious Freedom, and father of the University of Virginia.

With a background in corporate and nonprofit communications, Munson devotes her time now to writing and makes her home in Central Virginia. She lectures frequently on the Jefferson-Wythe legacy.

ENDNOTES

Chapter One
"A Deficit of Adequate Statesmen"

1 James Madison to Thomas Jefferson, 6 May 1780, *The Papers of James Madison*, vol. 2, (Chicago, 1962), p. 19-20.

2 George Washington to Benjamin Harrison, 18-30 December 1778, *The Papers of George Washington, Revolutionary War Series*, vol. 18, (Charlottesville, 2008), pp. 447-452.

3 Ibid.

4 An account of the banning of lawyers from Virginia's colonial courtrooms is contained in "Keep Your Eyes on the Bastards" by Robert Kirtland, *Toledo Law Review*, vol. 14, No 3, p. 689.

5 The Rev. Lee Massey, as quoted in *Old Churches, Ministers and Families of Virginia*, Bishop William Meade, vol. 1 (Philadelphia, 186), p. 238.

Chapter Two
America's First Leadership Training School

1 Thomas Jefferson, "Report of the Commissioners of the University of Virginia," 4 August 1818. (Char-

lottesville), University of Virginia. Special Collections.

2 Thomas Jefferson, "Bill for the More General Diffusion of Knowledge," 1-31 December 1778, *Quotes By and About Thomas Jefferson*, (Richmond).

3 Thomas Jefferson, "Letter to John Sanderson, Esq.," 31 August 1820. (Washington), Library of Congress.

4 Thomas Jefferson to Ralph Izard, 17 July 1788. (Washington), Library of Congress

5 Oscar Shewmake, "The Honourable George Wythe: Teacher, Lawyer, Jurist, Statesman," an address delivered before the Wythe Law Club of the College of William and Mary," (Williamsburg, 18 December 1921.

6 Lewis F. Powell, Jr., "Charter Day 1979: Justice Powell Describes Wythe as 'Fascinating Character,'" (Williamsburg 1979), p. 4.

7 Walker Maury to Thomas Jefferson, [ca.20 April 1784], *The Thomas Jefferson Papers*, Series One, (Washington), Library of Congress.

8 John Brown, in "William and Mary: America's First Law School," Fred B. Devitt Jr., *William & Mary Law Review*, Vol. 2, issue 2, article 8, p. 430.

9 Thomas Lee Shippen, in *The History of Legal Education in the United States*, Vol. 1, Steve Sheppard, ed.,

The Lawbook Exchange, Ltd., (Pasadena, CA 2006), p. 148.

10 William Munford to John Coalter, 24 April 1789, John Thompson Brown Papers, (Williamsburg) College of William and Mary.

11 John Coalter to Michael Coalter, 24 November 1789, in "Glimpses of Old College Life," *William and Mary College Quarterly*, (Williamsburg), January 1900.

12 Dice Robins Anderson, "The Teacher of Jefferson and Marshall," in *South Atlantic Quarterly* 15, no. 4 (October 1916), pp. 327-343.

13 "David McCullough: A Two-Time Pulitzer Prize Winner Who Loves His Wife, Family, History, and Is Simply a Nice Guy," The Huffington Post, May 26, 2015.

14 John Adams, Adams Family Papers, (Boston), Massachusetts Historical Society

15 George Wythe to John Adams, 5 December 1783, in *Papers of John Adams*, Vol. 15 (Cambridge, MA 1977), 396.

16 John Adams to George Wythe, *Adams Family Papers*, (Boston), Massachusetts Historical Society.

17 Abigail Adams, *Abigail Adams, Letters*, The Library of America (New York 2016).

18 Castellux, quoted in Clarkin, *Serene Patriot* (Al-

bany 1970), supra note 3, p. 149.

19 Richard Henry Lee to George Wythe, 28 February 1783, in *The Letters of Richard Henry Lee,* Vol 2, 1779-1794, ed. James Curtis Ballagh (Lexington, VA: Washington and Lee University), pp. 279-80.

20 *The American Gleaner* &c, Vol. 1, No. 1, Richmond, Saturday January 24, 1807.

21 Shewmake. Ibid.

Chapter Three
Leading Under the Constitution

1 James Madison, "Speech in Virginia Convention," 2 December 1829.

2 Henry Clay, as quoted in *American Patriotism: Speeches, Letters, and Other Papers,* compiled by Selim H. Peabody, (New York 1880), p. 489.

3 Patrick Henry, as quoted in *Encyclopedia of Virginia,* (Richmond), The Library of Virginia.

4 Oscar Shewmake, Ibid.

5 John Marshall, in *The Founders' Constitution,* University of Chicago, online.

6 Thomas Jefferson to James Madison, 15 March 1789, *Jefferson Papers,* Founders Online, (Washington), National Archives.

Chapter Four
Educating the Judges

1 John Adams, "Thoughts on Government," spring 1776, (Boston), Massachusetts Historical Society.

2 New World Encyclopedia, www.newworldency-clopedia.org/entry/George_Wythe

3 Thomas Jefferson, "Thomas Jefferson on Politics and Government," *The Papers of Thomas Jefferson*.

4 Judge Beverly Tucker, as quoted by B.B. Minor, *Decision of Cases in Virginia by the High Court of the Chancery*.

5 Anderson, Ibid.

6 Joyce Blackburn, *George Wythe of Williamsburg*, (New York 1975).

7 *American Gleaner*, Ibid.

8 The Rev. Charles A. Goodrich, *Lives of the Signers of the Declaration of Independence*.

9 Wythe's ruling in *Page v. Pendleton & Lyons* is covered in Wythe Holt's "George Wythe: Early Modern Judge," in *Alabama Law Review*, 58, no. 5 (2007), pp.1009-1039.

10 Hugh Grigsby, Discourse of the Life and Character of the Hon. Littleton Waller Tazewell, (Hamberg 2012).

11 Anderson, Ibid.

12 *Memoir, Correspondence, and Miscellanies from the Papers of Thomas Jefferson*, Vol. 1, Thomas Jefferson Randolph, ed., Boston, 1830.

13 Wythe Holt, Ibid.

14 William Munford, "Oration, Pronounced at the Funeral of George Wythe," (Richmond 1806).

Chapter Five
The Mentors

1 Thomas Jefferson to Jefferson Randolph, 24 November 1808, *The Writings of Thomas Jefferson*, (Princeton 1903).

2 Ibid.

3 Thomas Jefferson to William Duval, 14 June 1806, "The Thomas Jefferson Papers," Library of Congress.

4 Thomas Jefferson, "Letter to John Sanderson, Esq.," 31 August 1820, (Washington), National Archives.

5 Lewis F. Powell, Jr., "Charter Day 1979," Ibid.

6 William Wirt on Jefferson and Wythe: Eugene L Didier, "Thomas Jefferson as a Lawyer," *The Green Bag*, 15, no. 4 (April 1903), p. 158.

7 Henry Clay, in a speech regarding slavery, February 7, 1839.

8 Littleton Waller Tazewell, as quoted in *American Aristides*, Brown, (Rutherford), pp. 220-222.

9 George Wythe Munford, *The Two Parsons*, (Richmond), 1884.

10 The Reverend Charles A. Goodrich, *Lives of the Signers to the Declaration of Independence* (New York), 1856.

11 Thomas Jefferson to William Duval, Ibid.

Chapter Six
The Question of Slavery

1 Thomas Jefferson to Dr. Richard Price, 7 August 1785, *The Writings of Thomas Jefferson*, Vol. 5, Andrew A. Lipscomb, ed., (Washington, DC): The Thomas Jefferson Memorial Association, 1903, 55.

2 Thomas Jefferson to Jean Nicholas Demeunier, 26 June 1786, (Washington, DC): National Archives, Founders Archives.

3 Richard Randolph, in *Israel on the Appomattox: A Southern Experiment in Black Freedom from the 1790's Through the Civil War*, Melvin Patrick Ely, (New York, 2004)

4 Court case reviewed in *Pleasants v. Pleasants* and *Hudgins v. Hudgins, Wythe Holt*, "George Wythe: Early Modern Judge," *Alabama Law Review*, 1025-1036.

5 Descriptions of George Wythe's death generally rely on the account of George Wythe Munford, "Chancellor Wythe's Death," in *The Two Parsons*, (Richmond), 1884.

6 Shewmake, Ibid.

Chapter Seven
The Leadership Cohort

1 William Munford to John Coalter, 13 June 1790, "Glimpses of Old College Life," pp. 153-160.

2 Taylor Reveley, "Remembering a Long-Overlooked Signer of the Declaration of Independence," *Virginia Gazette News*, July 4, 2023.

3 Information about Wythe's students was drawn primarily from these sources: *The Dictionary of Virginia Biography*, the William & Mary Law Library *Wythepedia*, archives of the Library of Virginia, and numerous biographies.

DESCRIPTION OF SOURCES

Adams, Abigail, *Abigail Adams Letters*, Library Classics of the United States, Inc., New York: distributed by Penguin Random House, Inc., 2016.

Adams, John. *Diary and Autobiography of John Adams*, Lyman H. Butterfield et al, ed., Cambridge: Harvard University Press, 1961.

Adams, John. *The Political Writings of John Adams: Representative Selections*. George A. Peck, Jr., ed., Indianapolis: Hackett Publishing Company, Inc., 1954.

Anderson, Dice Robins. "The Teacher of Jefferson and Marshall," in *South Atlantic Quarterly* 15, no. 4 (October 1916), pp. 327-343.

Blackburn, Joyce. *George Wythe of Williamsburg*. New York: Harper & Row, 1975.

Brown, Imogene E., *American Aristides: A Biography of George Wythe*. Fairleigh Dickinson University Press, c. 1981.

Chadwick, Bruce. *I Am Murdered: George Wythe, Thomas Jefferson, and the Killing that Shocked a New Nation*. Hoboken: John Wiley & Sons, Inc., 2009.

Clarkin, William. *Serene Patriot: A Life of George Wythe*. Albany, New York: Alan Publications, 1970.

Clay, Henry. "Letter to B.B. Mino, Esq." In *Virginia*

Historical Register and Literary Companion 5, n. 3 (July 1852), 162-167.

Douglas, Davison M., "The Jeffersonian Vision of Legal Education," *Journal of Legal Education,* Vol. 51, No 2 (June 2001) pages 185-211.

Ely, Melvin Patrick. *Israel on the Appomattox.* New York: Random House, 2004.

Encyclopedia of Virginia. Richmond: The Library of Virginia, online.

Goodrich, Rev. Charles A. *Lives of the Signers of the Declaration of Independence,* New York: William Reed & Co., 1856.

Grigsby, Hugh. *Discourse of the Life and Character of the Hon. Littleton Waller Tazewell.* Hamberg, Germany: Tradition Classics, GmgH, 2012.

Holt, Wythe. "George Wythe: Early Modern Judge." In *Alabama Law Review* 58, no. 5 (2007): 1009-1039.

Jefferson Papers. Founders Online, Washington: The National Archives.

Jefferson, Thomas. "Letter to John Sanderson, Esq." 31 August 1820. Washington: Library of Congress.

Jefferson, Thomas. "Report of the Commissioners of the University of Virginia, 1818." Charlottesville: University of Virginia, Special Collections.

Jefferson, Thomas. *The Papers of Thomas Jefferson*, Julian P Boyd, ed. Princeton: Princeton University Press, 1953.

Jefferson, Thomas. *The Writings of Thomas Jefferson*, Andrew A. Lipscomb, ed., Washington D.C: The Thomas Jefferson Memorial Association, 1903.

Jefferson, Thomas. *Thomas Jefferson Writings*, Merrill D. Peterson, ed. New York: The Library of America, 1984.

Jefferson, Thomas. *Quotes By and About Thomas Jefferson*, Richmond: Dixon and Holt, 1784.

Madison, James. "From James Madison to Thomas Jefferson, 6 May 1780," *The Papers of James Madison*, *vol. 2*, Chicago: The University of Chicago Press, 1962.

Minor, B.B., "Memoir of the Author." In *George Wythe, Decisions of Cases in Virginia by the High Court of Chancery*. Richmond: J. W. Randolph, 1852.

Munford, George Wythe: *The Two Parsons*, Richmond: J.D.K.Slight, 1884.

Munford, William. "Glimpses of Old College Life," *William and Mary College Quarterly*, Williamsburg, January 1900.

Munford, William. "Oration, Pronounced at the Funeral of George Wythe." In *Richmond Enquirer,* June 13, 1806 and June 17, 1806.

Peabody, Selim H., editor. *American Patriotism: Speeches, Letters, and Other Papers*, New York: American Book Exchange, 1880, p. 489.

Powell, Lewis F., Jr., "Charter Day 1979: Justice Powell Describes Wythe as 'Fascinating Character.'" *William and Mary News*, Vol. VII, No. 20, 13 February 1979.

Randall, Willard Sterne. *Thomas Jefferson, A Life*, New York: Henry Holt and Company, 1993.

Reveley, W. Taylor III, "William & Mary Law School Came First. Why Care?" in *University of Toledo Law Review* 35 (2003), pages 185-188.

Shewmake, Oscar L., "The Honorable George Wythe: Teacher, Lawyer, Jurist, Statesman: "An Address Delivered Before the Wythe Law Club of the College of William and Mary in Williamsburg, Virginia, December 18, 1921," Richmond, Virginia, 1950.

Washington, George: "From George Washington to Benjamin Harrison, 18-30 December 1778, *The Papers of George Washington*, Revolutionary War Series, vol, 18, Charlottesville: University of Virginia Press, 2008, pp. 447-452.

Weems, M.L., "The Honest Lawyer, an Anecdote," *Charleston Times* (July 1, 1806), p. 3.

Made in the USA
Middletown, DE
27 September 2024